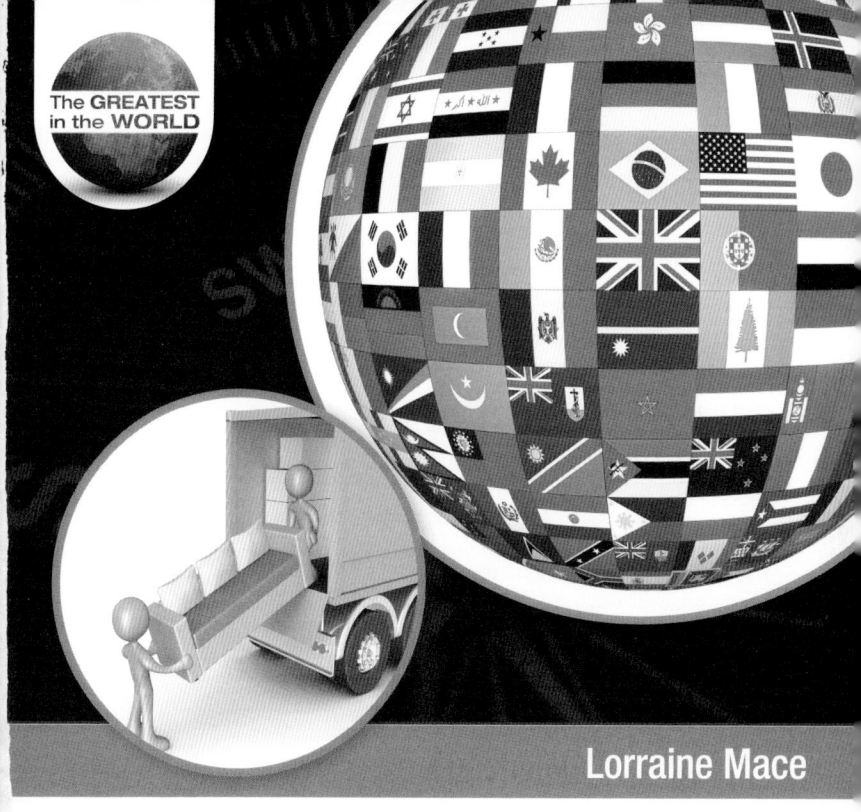

Lorraine Mace

The Greatest
Moving Abroad
Tips
in the World

A 'The Greatest in the World' book

www.thegreatestintheworld.com

Cover images:
© KTS Design; © Konstantinos Kokkinis
both courtesy of www.fotolia.com

Layout:
Shazia Saleemi
www.designspirit.co.uk

Copy editor:
Bronwyn Robertson
www.theartsva.com

Series creator/editor:
Steve Brookes

Published in 2008 by
The Greatest in the World Ltd, PO Box 3182,
Stratford-upon-Avon, Warwickshire CV37 7XW

A CIP catalogue record for this book is available from the British Library
ISBN 978-1-905151-47-9

Printed and bound in Italy by Printer Trento s.r.l.

This book is dedicated to the other two Musketeers, my wonderful children, David and Michelle, without whom my life wouldn't be complete. They were my travelling companions on my first few country hops (not that they had any say in the matter) and have since done a fair amount of relocating on their own.

I love them and I'm so proud of them that I'm a bore on the subject.

Foreword by Miranda Neame...

You're embarking on a move abroad... a life change. If moving house is considered one of the three most stressful events in a lifetime, moving to another country compounds the stress and the practical implications can seem daunting. But help is at hand! This book will help you to feel confident about the transition, making sure you don't forget any of the important considerations it will entail.

Perhaps you are fulfilling a dream or settling closer to family or making a career choice... whatever your motivation a move abroad is an exciting challenge, but it needs methodical planning and organisation. Lorraine Mace has made this easy, drawing on her own extensive experiences and observations, having been there, seen it, and done it eight times and in several continents.

In her book, future expatriates will find a comprehensive checklist for ensuring they pick the right location in the first place, that the move goes smoothly, and that they are prepared to face not only the practical aspects but also the psychological impact of living in a foreign country. No one willingly wants to be the subject of yet another hard-luck tale in the media and Lorraine methodically deals with the common misconceptions, mistakes and pitfalls before and after a move abroad.

Integrating into a foreign country is always enriching and mind-broadening but many people underestimate the depth and extent of the differences.

There may be a new language (or two) to grapple with, but in any case there will be the confrontation with an unknown culture, education, attitudes, etiquette, administrative structure, possibly a different state religion and code of ethics. It can take years, indeed a lifetime, to discover the deep-seated differences between your own culture and a foreign one.

Within Europe, France presents arguably the greatest culture shock a Briton is likely to experience in such a short trip from home, just a few miles across the Channel. Its customs, systems, values and language are so fundamentally opposite to Britain's. Yet one of the great joys of living here is the discovery and exchange of ideas. After living in France for more than 30 years, working and raising two children here, I am still finding out unsuspected secrets of French life, its history, geography, gastronomy, politics, mores and cultural references.

An open mind and a sense of humour are essential tools for integration. Even if you don't manage to master the language, anyone can learn the basic civilities (hello, thank you, goodbye, and so on) and your new neighbours are bound to appreciate your effort and they will probably enjoy your gaffes. A South African, an ardent conservationist and lover of nature, recently moved to France, was asked by her postman if she liked "naturisme". "Yes, absolutely", she enthused, and was very taken aback when he then brought out a sheaf of brochures for nudist holidays.

Often I hear from newcomers with problems stemming from an expectation that things will be done in the same way 'here' as 'at home'. So I can only agree with Lorraine: take nothing for granted and remember that you are the foreigner, not 'them'.

And there are some great advantages in being a foreigner. Most people, anywhere in the world, are hospitable to the stranger. Anyone who shows willing to accept new rules and customs will find a wealth of goodwill to help navigate the various challenges of business, property and inheritance laws, schooling and healthcare which Lorraine Mace covers here. One of the most frustrating aspects of adjusting to life in France, for example, is the administrative set-up, founded on entirely different principles from those in most Anglo-Saxon-based countries and dealt with in an entirely different way. Where there is a mix-up in the red tape, I always recommend going to speak to the relevant officials face to face. Almost invariably they are so pleased you have thrown yourself at their mercy that they will do all in their power to help.

And another thing, you shed your home identity as you leave your home country: you will be judged at face value; social status and background will not count for your new neighbours and colleagues – and this can be very liberating. You really can start a new life.

Good luck with it!

Miranda Neame

Editor, 'French News', France's English-language newspaper.

Contents

Choices, choices!

chapter 1
Choices, choices!

So you've decided to change your life by changing your country and are now running around like a headless chicken. So much to do and no one to tell you where to start, or even what should be on the list! Well, the most important thing is making the right choice about where to go. Even if your decision is made for you by a job offer, or you have family living abroad, you still need to be as certain as possible that the country is suitable for you. The more research you do before leaving, the easier it will be to settle into your new life.

Why on earth?

Now is the time, before making any life-changing decisions, to look critically at why you want to change country. You may well read that last sentence and think: "Oh, I know the answer to that!" and simply move on, but please don't. Honestly, there is a good reason why this tip is the first in the book.

Sit down, with your spouse if you have one, if not borrow someone else's because it's always useful to discuss things. Very often when thoughts are spoken out loud they have a habit of becoming more tangible. So, sit down with the spouse of your choice and write a list of the true reasons you want to live abroad. It doesn't matter what they are, as long as you are completely honest. Then, against each point, try to find a negative aspect.

At the end of this process you should have a realistic idea of why you want to make the move and also what you are looking for in your new country. This leads very neatly to...

Where on earth?

With so many places to choose from, how do you decide which one is right for you and your family? Well you could try sticking a pin in an atlas and hoping for the best, but you might end up at the North Pole, which isn't a great spot for sun-worshipers! A better idea is to make a shortlist of places you really like the sound of and then answer the questions below in respect of each. Less exciting I know, but much more effective.

- What are the legal requirements for residency?

- Is the cost of living within your means?

- Can you afford the type of property you want?

- Can you speak (or learn) the language?

- Is it possible to work?

- Is there enough to do if you don't work?

- Is the climate suitable?

- Is crime a problem?

- Will finding good schools be difficult?

- Is high-quality healthcare readily available?

Before you throw the idea (and this book) out of the window, don't panic! The tips that follow are designed to show you how to find the answers to all those questions and more.

What's the point?

For some countries it's more a question of do they want you? You might think anywhere you choose should welcome you with open arms, but that isn't always the case. Some of them are just picky, picky, picky! Australia, New Zealand, Canada, America and South Africa are very selective about which applicants are granted residency. Nor are they the only countries with strict entry criteria.

Many destinations operate a points system and it is essential to find out whether you qualify before making any life-changing decisions. Some embassies have websites where you can fill in an online form to calculate your points. Although much of Europe is now open, there are still restrictions on certain categories of residency. Take nothing for granted. Contact the embassy of your prospective country and ask for information.

Does your country need you?

Even countries that don't use a points system are not necessarily accepting immigrants with open arms. Unless you are moving to a country where you have automatic right of residence, there will be a variety of factors taken into account when you apply.

- Age is often a determining factor. Some countries are looking for young and able people to work in sectors where home-grown workers are in short supply. Other countries run schemes to attract retirees, offering advantageous tax breaks.

- Skills in certain professions and industries are welcome worldwide.

- The adaptability of spouses is also looked at very carefully (that's your own spouse, not the one you borrowed in the first tip!). Many years ago (shortly before my first ever move abroad) I attended a cocktail party at South Africa House – it was only much later that I realised it was a sneaky way of seeing how all the spouses were coping with the stress of the looming move.

- Language – in countries where there is more than one national language (for example, Canada, South Africa and the Maltese Islands) knowledge of the secondary official language counts greatly in your favour.

- Having a job to go to helps, but doesn't necessarily guarantee residency or a work permit.

- Having a clean police record. Not as straightforward as it sounds. Some countries look on unpaid parking fines as proof of a lawless attitude – so sort out those screwed up bits of paper from the back of the drawer and start writing some cheques.

Where's my job?

Even if you have an automatic right to live and work in a country, that won't mean a thing if there is a shortage of jobs. Most governments have statistics available showing unemployment figures.

Location, location, location

It isn't only estate agents that should keep that as a mantra to be repeated at every opportunity, but prospective expatriates should burn it on their brains.

Make a list of pluses and minuses for each of the countries that interest you. Be scrupulously honest, especially when it comes to the negative points. Moving abroad is incredibly expensive and even if you are going as a result of a job offer, and the company is paying all or part of the removal costs, the hidden costs could still cripple you financially if you decide to return to your home country. Often, assisted removal costs are reclaimed by the employer if the contract is broken before the full term, or a specified length of time, has passed.

Widen the net

There is nothing quite like firsthand testimony when trying to find out what it's really like living in a new and foreign environment. But, short of picking up the phone and calling all the English-looking names in the international directory, how do you get to talk to other expats? My tip would be to go online and join a few forums. You'll find many negative points are raised along with the positive.

If you're the shy and retiring type, it's better to find out that your potential neighbours are naturists before you settle on an area, than to have an eye-opening experience the first time you visit the beach.

You'll find some good places to start an online search in the lists section at the end of the book.

Nearest and dearest

Take into account the time and cost involved in being able to see your family and friends on a regular basis. The further away you move the more expensive it becomes for the exchange of visits. The world is a smaller place than it used to be, but it still takes hundreds of pounds and more than fourteen hours to get from one side to the other.

Telephone contact becomes more difficult when taking time zones into account, particularly when one of you is in yesterday and the other one is calling from tomorrow.

Online is not real life

No matter how diligent you are with your online searches and exchanges of information, nothing beats going to see for yourself. Inspection trips are a vital part of the decision making process and, if possible, you should go for two or three months before making a final choice of where to settle.

All properties great and small

What is the cost of housing? Would you be able to afford your dream home, or would you have to settle for something smaller and with neighbours much closer than you are used to?

On the other hand, the properties available might mean your nearest neighbour is three miles away. If you've been accustomed to chatting over a garden fence you'll either need to invest in a loud hailer or get used to solitude.

Inspecting the inspection trips

There are many companies that specialise in short viewing trips for prospective immigrants. Whilst this may be the cheapest option for your initial inspection, do bear in mind you will only be taken to those areas that show the country in its best possible light. You need to spend time away from the salesperson who is showing you around, and explore the area on your own.

Roaming and phoning

It's a good idea to buy a cheap mobile phone, or get a local SIM card, to use while on your inspection trips. Using a mobile abroad runs up enormous costs in roaming charges. The call you make to the estate agent, or to book a table at a restaurant, goes from Foreignland back to your home country and then gets diverted back to Foreignland again, notching up charges every time it passes through a network.

The other beauty of organising a mobile phone in your intended country is that you can give the number to family and friends before you leave.

Read all about it

Find out if there is an English-language newspaper available. Most countries with an expat population have at least one. Reading this will give you a better idea of what the political climate is really like, where the crime rates are highest, if there are problems with local government corruption or infrastructure concerns due to the sudden influx of immigrants.

The true cost of living

Estate agents and other interested parties would have you believe the cost of living is so low you can live like a king on a quarter of your current income – and they could be telling the truth, but how can you find out? This is another great reason for signing on to a few expat websites. If you have made up your mind where to go, you can find out the true cost of food, utilities and other regular expenses such as local taxes. If you are trying to decide between two countries, you can make comparisons based on the experiences of those actually living in those countries.

Pocketing the difference

Once you've found out what it would cost to live in your preferred destination, you need to see if you can afford it. Financial insecurity could destroy any enjoyment you might otherwise have in your new home.

Set out your finances and decide if it is possible to live on no more than three-quarters of your income. Apart from giving a more realistic view of affordability, the difference could be your rainy day money. This could help towards evening out any future currency fluctuations, or even provide the finance to return home if your dream turns into a nightmare.

Extra, extra, spend all about it!

The costs of moving abroad can seem endless. In fact, if you don't list all the items upfront, you could discover too late that your finances cannot extend that far.

- Exploration trips – don't skimp on them, they could be the difference between being happy in paradise or miserable in perpetuity.

- Relocation costs – fares for you, your family and the pets, including any stopovers, such as months in quarantine (the pets, not you).

- Transporting your worldly goods and insuring them in case they go to Austria and you go to Australia.

- Visas – the country may want you, but they'll still make you pay.

- New furniture, carpets and other essentials.

- Private healthcare, if needed.

- Upfront housing costs, such as two or three months' rent, connection fees for services and utilities.

- Agent's fees – in many countries you pay an agency fee for finding you somewhere to rent.

- Legal fees.

- Accountancy fees.

- School fees.

Schools of thought

Generally speaking, children under the age of twelve seem to adapt much better than teenagers, but, regardless of age, care must be taken to ensure the move is as easy for them as possible.

Things to consider:

- Language – do you put your child into a local language school or try to find an English alternative?

- How difficult would it be for your child to be taught entirely in a foreign language?

- Are government schools (regardless of language considerations) providing the standard of education you want?

- Are private schools within your budget?

- If yes, is a private school close enough to commute each day?

- Is commuting safe?

- What are the additional costs of schooling, government and/or private, such as books, sports equipment and uniforms?

- Will your village-educated child cope with an inner-city school, or vice versa?

Permitted to learn?

If you are taking children abroad, one of the essential pieces of research will concern schooling. Do find out as soon as possible whether your visa or work permit allows your children to attend school. Very often admittance depends on the parents' visas.

Home school

For many countries the only consideration taken into account is that the child receives a balanced education. Providing you can satisfy the authorities of your ability to do so, you can educate your child at home.

This could be particularly helpful if your child has learning difficulties or other special needs and you find the local schools cannot cater for your requirements.

One possible downside to home education is that the child misses out on the opportunity to integrate with others of their age group.

Don't get bowled out

If playing a sport, such as cricket, is a major part of your leisure time, don't forget to make sure there are maidens to be bowled over. Some sports are truly international, but others won't feature in your new destination. Do some research into the sporting activities of the local population and decide whether the new challenges on offer will compensate for what you might have to give up. You never know, providing you survive, crocodile wrestling could be every bit as enjoyable as lawn bowls.

When they grow up

Are there plenty of jobs for the young local population, or are the graduates leaving in droves to find work abroad? If that is the case it could mean your own children will leave once they have completed their education. It may be several years before you have to face the problem, but do bear it in mind in your decision making.

Culturally speaking

Do you enjoy going to the cinema or theatre? How much would it matter to you if there were not any cultural activities in English? What about other activities, such as going to watch football matches, trips to the pub or horseracing? How much would you miss any of those? Bingo is not necessarily available everywhere in the world and, even if it is played, it might not resemble the version you are used to. Imagine winning the major house of the night and taking home half a pig and three live chickens.

Culture clashing

Open your eyes to the cultural activities of the locals, even (or especially) if it is something you don't wish to see. The populace will have been carrying out their sports for centuries and the activity will be discussed, written about in the press, shown on television and have posters on every street corner when one of the events comes to town. For example, if bullfighting upsets you, don't go to Spain. If shooting migrating birds by the hundreds distresses you, don't go to the Maltese Islands.

Islands in the sun

Living on an island sounds wonderful, and it can be exactly that, but there is an aspect of island living that shouldn't be ignored. Getting to and from the nearest mainland is an additional cost factor. How regular are ferries, helicopter or other services to enable you to get to the closest international airport?

Have the expats formed a closed 'island mentality' community? Would you fit into the social scene? If not, you must consider the alternatives.

Paradise found

Make yourself a tick list of all the things the new country must have, a second list of those it would be nice to have, and a third list of those aspects which would add an extra dimension to your standard of living.

Against that make another list of all the things you can find out that you don't like about either the country or its people. Compare the lists and see if you can find your own little corner of the world you would consider paradise.

Things that go hiss in the night

Rose-tinted glasses are great for holidays and short business trips, but, if you are planning to live in an area, the glasses need to come off. There could be any number of wonderful reasons for choosing your destination, but if the mere idea of a giant spider, slithery snake, or poisonous toad brings you out in a cold sweat, then living in an environment where any of them can drop in for a visit is not for you.

Political reality

Government and local corruption is endemic in certain countries. In fact, in some places bribery isn't regarded as corrupt, merely a necessary greasing of the wheels of power. So, if your chosen country needs monetary sweeteners every step of the way and the thought of that turns you sour, then my advice is simple – don't go there. They will not change their customs and way of life for you, regardless of how helpful you think it would be to free the people from the tyranny of political corruption.

It's criminal what you can find out

Check out the crime figures. Is a drug culture responsible for petty crime? This is something often hidden from tourists, but can be ascertained from online searches. Start by going to the website of the *United Nations Interregional Crime and Justice Research Institute*: http://www.unicri.it.

A serpent next door to Eden

On the subject of politics, you may think local—or even national—politics are nothing to do with you, but you might find they touch your life more than you would like. Do some research into the political situation, not just the country you intend to move to, but also the neighbouring nations. Wars, riots, military coups and civil unrest can play havoc with a peaceful Sunday afternoon barbeque.

Paradise lost

Paradise can also play up a bit with the weather. Does your Garden of Eden suffer periodic hurricanes, earthquakes or annual floods? Or is there any chance of losing your home beneath a few kilograms of molten ash from a nearby active volcano?

Take a reality check

One of the reasons for moving abroad is to experience a different way of living. Don't expect things to be the same with better weather, because life doesn't work like that. If there are certain aspects of your existence in your home country you simply cannot live without, and you know you will not be able to replicate those things abroad, then regardless of how trivial they may seem to your spouse, or anyone else, dig your heels in and don't go.

Advance to go

Some of the tips in this chapter might seem as though I'm saying stay put and don't move abroad. That isn't meant to be the case at all, but if you go with your eyes wide open to all the possible downsides, you'll be better equipped to cope with the challenges of moving to a strange country.

The important thing is to enjoy the whole experience. Make a game of the planning and organising. Moving to a new country is a massively exciting adventure, so do find time to follow the most important tip of all – to have fun!

Summary:

- Be honest about your reasons for moving abroad. Ignoring qualms could result in a costly mistake.

- Calculate your finances very carefully. If in doubt, don't go.

- Take into account all the negative factors about your choice of country, not just the positive and appealing ones.

- Once you've decided where to go make sure your circumstances make you acceptable to the country.

- Put plans in place that make it easy to stay in touch with friends & family.

- Visit expatriate websites, join forums, ask questions. If you can't get the answers on one site, join another.

- Find out the true cost of living in the new country. Don't take interested parties' word for it.

- Take into account schooling needs for your children, and also the possible language problems and job opportunities.

- Boredom is a killer of happiness so make sure there are leisure activities available to spend your free time on.

- If cultural events are important to you now, do remember they will still be important when you move.

- Look at the political situation very carefully, including neighbouring countries. Check out local crime figures.

- If you can't bring yourself to get rid of a spider from the bath, then check out the local wildlife.

Moving times

chapter 2
Moving times

You've chosen the country and they've accepted you, so that's the end of any problems. Right? Wrong! It is at this point that it begins to sink in that you've committed yourself to a period of intense lunacy. But don't panic, take a deep breath instead, and then read the following tips.

Removing the removal stress

- Check local prices of electrical goods as buying new can be cheaper than shipping existing appliances.

- Conversely, you might find it cheaper to buy new appliances in your home country, or even discover that goods you take for granted, such as a dishwasher, are not available at all in your new location.

- Find out if properties are sold furnished.

- Remember that new developments in many countries have fitted kitchens.

- If downsizing, look critically at your possessions – will the baby grand piano really fit in a room a third of the size you have now?

Going, going, gone – not you, your surplus belongings

Long before you call in anyone to give you a quote for transporting your belongings to their new home, you should go through the house from top to bottom writing a list and pricing everything you don't want.

A car boot sale (or a yard sale in US parlance) is an ideal opportunity to make some extra cash while ridding your life of all the surplus rubbish that I bet you're hoarding in every nook and cranny.

The first time I moved abroad I took every item I possessed, on the basis that it might come in handy one day. Five countries and nine moves later, I've learned my lesson and if an item hasn't been used since the last move, it doesn't get on the removal van.

This period is a great opportunity to clear out the clutter. Ask yourself if the pasta-making machine you bought in a fit of enthusiasm after a romantic holiday in Rome, but which has never shaped dough, is really needed for your new life in Outer Mongolia. The chances are you'll find many items that have never seen the light of day and, with the high cost of international removal, second-cousin Jane's ugly china vase becomes an expensive keepsake.

Customs to excise the mind

The most amazing things can be found on lists of forbidden imports. Australia, for example, bans pot pourri, straw objects and dirty walking boots, to name just a few of the more bizarre items. But even if all of your goods and chattels are on the allowed list, you might want to reconsider packing up your entire home when faced with exorbitant excise charges. That fine wine collection might be better given away as parting gifts because many countries charge a fairly hefty import duty.

Most countries have restrictions on importing plants of any kind, so find good homes for all your houseplants. To find out what can be taken into your chosen country your first port of call should be the official government website. From the homepage you should be able to find the rules and regulations relating to imported goods and livestock.

Here, there or anywhere?

The chances are high that you'll need to put your furniture and personal effects into storage for a period of time. Before you wave farewell to all your worldly goods, make a list of the items you cannot live without, not even for a few weeks. You really don't want to be wishing you'd kept the super-effective mosquito net handy when being eaten alive by hungry flying insects. The cost of storage can vary greatly. Check whether it is cheaper at home or in the new destination. The larger international movers have their own facilities, but, although convenient, this is not always the most economical option. Ask if insurance is included as it is sometimes cheaper to go with a higher quote once the insurance factor is taken into account.

Visas, permits and other important stuff

How much time does it take for visas and permits to be issued? This is another question for those wonderful folk on the expats' websites. Official sources may well say visas are issued within four months, but often personal experience says otherwise and perhaps six, eight, or even ten months should be allowed.

Size matters

Don't take it for granted that the multiple photographs you will be asked to supply for visas and other official documents will be standard passport photo size. The requirements can vary from country to country and even differ between departments within a country. Ask the question before you have the pictures taken.

The ghost of passport past

It is possible that you will need to have a passport which is valid for at least six months when you apply for visas, residence or work permits. If you are within six to nine months of your passport expiring it's a good idea to get it extended before making any applications.

Getting the needle

If your chosen country requires vaccinations against endemic diseases you need to plan the timing of these very carefully. Very often the immunisations need to be given within certain time frames.

It's all in the planning

At the first available opportunity after deciding on your country of choice you need to plan your move. This is where you find out how much time it takes for the immunisations, visas, removal quotes, clearing customs and all the other million and one things you are going to have to organise.

Start by making a month by month pad and jotting down everything that needs to happen in each particular month, allowing sufficient time for each phase. Every time a new piece of information comes in you add it to the right month on your makeshift calendar.

The next thing to do is to put more detail into the planning. Either set up a spreadsheet on your computer, or use a page a day diary to organise each month. Transfer the information from the monthly lists to the daily pages. Put *everything* down, regardless of how trivial it may seem. Believe me, it won't seem trivial when you realise your only suit is still in the dry cleaners in Bradford, but you are in Brisbane about to attend your first day at work.

Work your plan

Mark off each aspect as it is completed. If it is only partially done, or the date has to be moved, then put the changed details on the monthly chart and also on the day-by-day plan.

Make new lists as you go of all the things you realise need to be with you when you travel, or that you will need access to soon after arrival.

Keep all your important papers, birth certificates, marriage certificates, proof of education, visas, vaccination papers, international driving licence, permits—in fact anything you might be asked for—in one file.

Decide who is going to be in charge of tickets, passports and currency and stick with the decision. If one of these items is needed it is up to the person responsible to hound their partner to distraction until the missing document is safely back where it belongs. Arriving at the airport to find one of the passports or tickets has gone astray because someone took it out of the file and forgot to put it back is more than just slightly annoying — missing your flight is not a recipe for happy families abroad.

It's in the bag

If there are items you think might be difficult to source straight away, such as coffee filters or vacuum cleaner bags, buy before you go and pack them.

Cash in hand

Buy some local currency and become accustomed to the look and feel of it. You acquire a friend for life when you tip the taxi driver £50 instead of the equivalent of £5 as you intended, but that isn't going to help you keep to your budget.

One way of getting used to the values of foreign notes is to play monopoly, or another money-based board game, with them.

Have you used this company?

Regardless of how charming the gentleman from the removal company is, or how efficient the lady seems to be, always get at least three quotes for removals. Ask for references and call them. Even if it means staying up until four in the morning to speak to someone in Australia, call the references. It's really the only way to find out if your precious treasures will be in safe hands.

Broker a better deal

Sometimes it is possible to get a better price for removals if the company concerned has just moved someone to your home country and would otherwise be taking an empty container or lorry back again, but how do you find these people in need of your goods? Try doing an online search for removal companies in the country you are moving to, or alternatively, try one of the removal brokers listed below. They take your details, send them out to various companies and come back to you with the best price. But, as above, ask for references and follow up on them.

You should still get quotes from firms locally, but you might be able to take advantage of the empty return syndrome and get a better price.

www.etbrokers-removals.com

www.removalbroker.co.uk

www.removalsbrokers.co.uk

www.rbww.com.au

www.removalbrokersaustralia.com.au

Parking and marking

Is there enough room for a lorry to park outside your property? Packing for an overseas move takes much longer than it does for a local one. It can take two or three days for the job and you need to make sure local regulations allow you to have a lorry parked outside for that length of time.

If traffic problems are likely to occur as a result, you need to contact the local authorities to arrange a permit. Ask your removal company for assistance in deciding how much room is required and for how long.

Inventing the inventory

This is one of the most tedious of all the jobs you'll need to complete prior to moving abroad, but it has to be done, so the sooner you get down to it the better you'll feel.

You need to list all the items you'll be shipping abroad and their replacement values. This list will have a variety of uses, so make plenty of copies. It will be needed for:

- Calculating any import duties that might have to be paid.

- Insurance quotes for shipping and storage.

- To be shown by the shipper at border points.

Apart from the above, you should keep a copy for yourself to note which items have gone into which boxes. This will help tremendously when your goods arrive and you find you cannot live a second longer without listening to the CD which, because you've been clever, you know is packed in box 27.

" Never mistake motion
for action. ”

Ernest Hemingway (1899 - 1961)

Ticking all the boxes

If at all possible, it is a good idea to be present when your container is opened for the customs inspection. You know your goods best of all and can answer any questions that might arise.

Not all countries require this, it depends where you are coming from and going to. Your shipping agent will advise you if your goods need to clear customs at final destination.

Batteries

Remove batteries from all appliances before packing. If the appliance still has its original box you can slip the batteries in with it, otherwise tape them to the side of the appliance.

Expat trivia

According to the Institute for Public Policy Research over 25% of expats moved abroad to improve their lifestyle and enjoy better weather. The same survey found that 18% gave family as a key reason for relocating. Education and professional opportunities accounted for another 34% – with Canada coming high on the list of countries fulfilling these criteria.

So long, it's been good to know you

Don't forget to tell the following that you are moving. You may well think of even more:

- Banks
- Blood bank
- Book clubs
- Car insurance/breakdown cover/registration
- Catalogue companies
- Credit card companies
- Dentist
- Doctor
- Electoral register
- Electricity/gas/heating oil providers (take readings for final accounts)
- Friends – local and overseas
- Football pools
- Gym membership/sports clubs
- Inland Revenue
- Insurance companies and agents
- Internet service provider
- Library

- Local council
- Magazine subscriptions
- Milk delivery service
- National health insurance
- Newspaper shop
- Optician
- Pharmacy
- Private healthcare companies
- Private pension companies
- Professional associations
- RAC, AA, or other motoring organisation
- Relatives – local and overseas
- Rental and/or hire purchase companies
- Schools
- Store cards
- Telephone/mobile phone
- TV licence
- Unions
- Vet
- Water company (take reading for final account)
- Window cleaner

Mail forwarding

Regardless of how well you organise your list, there is bound to be someone you forget to notify. For this reason, as well as for your own peace of mind, it is worth taking out a mail redirection subscription with the Post Office.

Forward thinking

Even if you do not have a definitive address to go to, you will still need to give a forwarding address to the Post Office and those on the list above, to say nothing of your nearest and dearest. Ask a local estate agent on one of your inspection trips to assist you in opening a post office box. If this is not possible, ask if you can have mail forwarded to the agency as an interim measure until you get things sorted.

Forward planning

Unless you have bought or rented somewhere in your chosen location, you need to give yourselves as much time as possible to find the right place to rent. Book a hotel in advance for at least three days to give you some breathing space.

Key points

Gather up all the spare keys for cars, house, caravan, safety deposit box, business, clubs and lockers. Label them and put them all in one place, a drawer is a good idea, so that when the time comes to hand them over you will know exactly where to look. This might sound ridiculous, but the chances are quite high that a few weeks into the moving process you won't even remember where you live, far less where the spare keys are.

Organise and prioritise

It's list time again – I know, I can hear you groaning, but the more lists you make, the easier the move becomes. Make a list of 'must-haves'. This time you need to think carefully about what you'll need when you first arrive. Anything that is essential to you, that you or your family cannot do without for several weeks, should go with you in your luggage. Even if this means paying for excess baggage, pay it. If the items are that important, now is not the time to skimp on cost.

Make a second list of those items you won't need straight away, but that will be required within a few weeks. Arrange to have those items sent by courier, or by surface mail. Everything else goes on the inventory list for the shipping company.

Get it all online

Delays in receiving credit card or bank statements could cause financial penalties, so get it all online before you go. Once online accounts are set up they can be accessed from any computer anywhere in the world, but only by you or someone to whom you have given your security details.

Open an email account such as hotmail that you can use until you have established yourself in your new country. Again, this can be accessed anywhere.

Paper, paper, everywhere

Photocopy every piece of important paper you possess. You'll need several copies of everything, namely: birth certificates, marriage certificates, divorce papers, passports, visas, permits of any kind, driving licences. If it is official, essential or precious, then copy it – again and again. You can never have too many photocopies.

Shred it

In the clearing out process you should rid your home of excess paper; otherwise you'll be paying to ship boxes of rubbish to your new home. If you don't already have one, now is the time to buy a paper shredder. Go through all your old paperwork and shred everything you don't need – bank statements, credit cards bills, anything that contains your personal information.

If you are doing your own packing, the shredded paper makes wonderful packing material for fragile items.

Expat trivia

According to the latest official figures (2006) there are six British pensioners living in Cuba. Only two expat pensioners are recorded as living in Mongolia. Three are known to be resident in Tahiti. There are none registered in North Korea.

Summary:

- Clear out the clutter. Get rid of all the unwanted gifts, bargain buys and unused objects.

- Sort out visas, permits and other paperwork. Don't forget to check passports haven't expired, or are close to expiry.

- Make lists of everything you need to do, remember or check. Make a list of all the things you need to make lists for.

- Make a long-term plan and a series of short-term plans. Move unfinished items to the next month.

- Get used to the value of the new foreign currency, so that you are ready to purchase items, or pay taxi fares on arrival.

- Get several quotes for removal and storage and ensure they include the cost of insurance.

- Make an inventory as soon as possible to calculate storage, insurance and possible import duties.

- Notify all key people that you are moving abroad and those in your new country who need to know you are arriving.

- Organise your bank and credit card accounts so that you can access them and your statements online.

- Make multiple photocopies of all your important papers. If they are official you'll need copies – lots of them!

- Keep all keys in a safe place and labelled clearly so that you don't inadvertently give the wrong keys.

- Shred anything that has your personal information on and can be used to steal your identity.

MOVING

Pets & vets

chapter 3
Pets & vets

Taking your animals with you when you move abroad can be almost as costly as all the rest of your move's expenses combined. But if you decide the pain of leaving them behind is too great, and choose to relocate with your hairy, furry or feathery friends, it requires careful planning.

Timing is all

Depending on your new country's requirements, it can be a complex business to gather together all the documentation required and make sure examinations and vaccinations are given at the correct time. You should allow at least six months prior to the actual leaving date, to organise everything.

The first point of contact should be the embassy/consulate of your chosen country, or your own embassy/consulate in your country of destination, to ascertain exactly what the rules are for relocating pets. Most embassies have online information, but if they don't, an email or phone call is essential to ask for a list of regulations and guidelines.

When is a pet not a pet?

The short answer to that question is when the country of destination says so. Some countries regard certain breeds of dog as undesirable, won't accept reptiles, or have strict import regulations regarding birds. Sometimes an animal will be acceptable from one country of origin, but not from another – the only way to be sure if your beloved friend is allowed into your chosen country is to ask for a list of banned animals.

Just passing through

On some long-haul destinations it will be necessary for your pets to pass through other countries en route, to change aircraft, or even to stop overnight. If you are organising the travel arrangements yourself, do check the regulations of all countries concerned, or you might find Fido held up while paperwork and regulations are sorted out.

Innocent of any crime – but still behind bars

Many countries operate a quarantine scheme, especially those where diseases such as rabies have been eradicated. If your animals are reasonably young this shouldn't present too much of a problem, even though it is heartbreaking to know they are being locked away for a period of time. But if your pets are old and close to the end of their lives, it is worth asking yourself if you could stand the pain of losing them while they are still in quarantine. If there is a real chance of this happening, you might want to look at ways of putting off the move for a few months.

Using a pet transport service

A pet transport service will take many of the travel arrangements off your hands, but the cost will be high. Even so, if you can afford it, having someone else deal with the regulations will give you more time to sort out your pet's vaccinations and other requirements.

Pet transport questions

- Does the estimate include door to door (or quarantine) delivery service?

- Are there any additional costs to take into account?

- Will they give you a complete list of all certificates and other documentation you need to complete?

- Will they give you a timetable of when you need to arrange vet's examinations and vaccinations to meet your destination country's requirements?

- Do they organise import permits?

- Do they arrange boarding prior to shipping and on landing, if required?

- Do they use non-stop flights wherever possible?

- On long-haul journeys what arrangements do they make for stopovers?

- Do they have arrangements with their agents in other countries to keep track of pets every step of the journey?

- Will they give you exact instructions regarding food to supply for the journey and when to feed your pet prior to travelling?

Get several quotes and compare them. You need to be happy that your family friend is in the best possible hands.

Bedding in

One way to lessen the trauma for an animal is to purchase the travelling crate a few months before the date of departure and let your pet use it as its regular place to sleep. Put tasty titbits inside so that it becomes a place of enjoyment, enabling your pet to relax.

Leave the door open until they are completely comfortable with going in and out. If it is possible, once they are acclimatised, it's a good idea to take your pets out in their travelling containers. The more familiar they are with their travelling environment, the less traumatic the move will be for them.

Feeling hot, hot, hot!

You may feel that putting plenty of blankets in their container will make them more comfortable during the journey, but dogs in particular suffer if they are too hot. A dog will curl up and keep itself warm in cold conditions, but will find it almost impossible to cool down if too many blankets are in the way.

Ask for your vet's advice about appropriate bedding, taking into account the end destination, the journey itself, and the breed of dog.

Lassie, come home

If life abroad doesn't work out for you, it would be wonderful to be able to come back without your pets needing to go into quarantine. The only way to ensure this is the case is to take every precaution before you leave.

If your country of *origin* is the UK you should contact the Department for Environment, Food and Rural Affairs, **www.defra.gov.uk/animalh/quarantine/index.htm**, for advice on what to do *before* leaving and what to do in your new country of residence, to enable your pet to return to the UK without being quarantined.

Defra
Customer Contact Unit
Eastbury House
30 - 34 Albert Embankment
London SE1 7TL

Email: helpline@defra.gsi.gov.uk

Telephone: 08459 335 577

From outside the UK the Helpline telephone number is:
+44 (0) 20 7238 6951

If you are moving to the USA with an animal, you should contact the United States Department of Agriculture, Animal and Plant Health Inspection Service, **www.aphis.usda.gov/vs/ncie/pet-info.html**

Veterinary Services
National Centre For Import And Export
Import/Export Animals
4700 River Road, Unit 39
Riverdale, MD 20737-1231

Phone: +001 (301) 734-3277

Taking stock

Providing it doesn't contravene the rules of your country of destination, it's a good idea to take a supply of flea tablets, worming remedies and other regularly used products. When you have only just moved, particularly if English isn't the language spoken in the shops, needing something to ward off fleas could catch you on the hop.

Ticking all the options

In many countries your pets will encounter ticks and other parasites or diseases not endemic to their country of origin and, as a result, may not have a natural resistance to them. Talk to your vet and ask advice on what you can do as a preventative measure, or, if that isn't an option, what signs you should look for in terms of symptoms.

PETS – pet travel scheme

Many countries around the world now operate the PETS passport system, which allows for the unrestricted movement of certain domestic animals. To find out whether or not your new country has signed up to the scheme visit the Defra website at the following address:
www.defra.gov.uk/animalh/quarantine/factsheet/factsheet.htm.

Expat trivia

More than 9 million emigrants left Liverpool between 1830 and 1930.

You're the foreigner

chapter 4
You're the foreigner

A good point to bear in mind is that the natives aren't foreign, you are! They may speak funny, eat strange foods and have odd customs, but only in your eyes. To them, you're the one acting weird, but it needn't be like that. You can learn to speak funny, become more adventurous in your dining habits (even if it means eating with your eyes closed) and join in.

Lingo learning in advance

Even if all you can say is hello, goodbye or ask how someone is, those few words could make an enormous difference to how you are received by the locals. Before you pack up your home and wave farewell to your home country, try to learn how to say hello to the new one. Whether you are doing it in English, Mandarin or Portuguese, as the incomer it will be up to you to make the first move socially. Smile and say hello.

How many languages do they speak here?

As soon as the goods are unpacked and home feels like home it's time to venture into the world outside. Even when English is one of the official languages in your new country, as in, for example, South Africa, Malta and Gibraltar, learning one of the other languages will help you to integrate and make new friends. Contact the local equivalent of the town council and ask if they offer language classes – often these are supplied at little or no cost to immigrants.

Get clubbing!

Sports and leisure activities transcend language and cultural barriers. Whether you are playing chess in Chile, tennis in Transylvania or practising your archery in Australia, joining a club gets you talking and mixing with the local population. Even if you have never played a sport or been involved in leisure activities, now is a good time to start. Don't sit at home feeling isolated, get out clubbing!

Talking TV

A great way of improving fluency in a foreign language is through watching the television. Long programmes will be beyond you at first, but don't lose heart. Change the way you watch TV. Back home you might have found the commercials the best time to make a quick cup of tea, but in Foreignland they become prime-time viewing. The messages are short and visual; making it easy to understand what is going on. Also, the language is more likely to reflect current usage, so you'll find it easier to understand when your neighbours use words not found in your English/Foreign dictionary.

Reading TV

Many of the quiz programmes you know and love (or loathe) are broadcast worldwide. Quizzes where the questions are shown on screen are a great aid to increasing vocabulary. Just think how impressed you'll be with yourself when you can shout: "It's 'B', stupid!" in Swahili, unless, of course, you're living in Sweden!

Shall we dance?

Dance classes are a great way of meeting people, as well as a way of getting (or keeping) fit. If language is an issue, line-dancing might be the way to go. Copying everyone else at a beginners' class is easy enough to do and doesn't require too much talking – but do remember to learn how to say "I'm sorry", ready for when you crunch someone's toes.

Feeling the physical pull

Homesickness can manifest itself as physical symptoms. You might suffer more colds than usual, or feel unwell in other ways, such as headaches, nausea or depression. This is perfectly normal! The 'fright' stage, where you feel you simply want to up sticks and go home can attack once the honeymoon phase is over, but don't panic – it passes, and soon you'll wonder why on earth you were upset.

Homesick blues-beater – part one

Everyone feels some degree of homesickness and it's important to realise that this is a normal response to moving abroad. The best way of dealing with it is to constantly remind yourself of all the things you like about your new environment. Keep a notebook and every evening record at least three things you enjoyed about that day. It doesn't matter if you list some items several times over, you'll simply reinforce your positive attitude to that particular aspect of your new life.

Homesick blues-beater – part two

Make regular times to call friends and family. Keeping in touch by phone and email will stop you from feeling as though you have been cut off from your previous life. Let everyone know how your life is changing. At the same time, keep up to date with the important things in their lives. The more time that passes between phone calls or emails, the harder it is to talk about the day-to-day things that help to maintain relationships.

The way we were… not!

During periods of homesickness it is very easy to remember the life you've left behind as being better in every way than it really was. Keep a list of all the reasons why you wanted to move abroad in the first place and refer to it when you start remembering life back home as perfect.

Making a fist of things

Study the hand gestures of your neighbours and actors on television soaps, particularly if they are enraged about something. Keep in mind the television advertisement for a worldwide bank where they pointed out all the ways in which different races use non-verbal signals. You'll be amazed at how something that is regarded as inoffensive or funny at home can be insulting abroad. Keep your hands as still as possible until you are sure you won't be making a fist of things.

Cooking up a storm

Buy an illustrated cookery book of the local cuisine and practise the dishes at home. This will not only help with reading in a foreign language and enable you to get to know the dishes of the country, but it will also make it easier for you to eat out. If you've already seen in your recipe book that a particular dish is made from grated snail's intestines, you'll know not to order it, unless, of course, you are feeling really adventurous.

And now for a bedtime story

Reading foreign books and newspapers is hard when your vocabulary is limited. Why not buy a couple of children's books, preferably ones you've either read in English as a child or read to your own children? Knowing the gist of the story will help you to understand what is going on and stop you from reaching for the dictionary every second word.

Another good source of reading material is the local version of the TV Times, or any of the celebrity magazines. These contain plenty of pictures and short news items written in a modern style, giving you plenty of colloquial usage.

Community service

Go along to the local council offices and put your name down as a volunteer. It doesn't matter what you do, whether it's visiting the sick, making cakes for local fiestas, selling raffle tickets or planting bulbs, every time you volunteer it introduces you to new people, improves your language skills and forces you to communicate with your community.

Shop 'til you drop

Explore the shopping scene – not just the larger shopping centres, where they are more likely to have English-speaking staff, but the local markets and smaller independent shops. Practise asking for prices and quantities before setting out on your trip. The more you chat to local shopkeepers, the quicker you'll feel comfortable using your new language skills.

Consuming issues – part one

If there are products from home that you really don't want to do without, try doing an online search. In today's rapidly shrinking world online shops are available for almost every commodity. You may have to pay three or four times the price you are used to, but if having a particular bottle of sauce, or relaxing in a much-loved bath product, helps you to settle in your new home, it's most probably worth the additional cost.

Consuming issues – part two

Invite your new neighbours for a meal, something traditional to your home country that they are unlikely to have tried before. Sharing your cultural background opens up new avenues of conversation – but do remember, a reciprocal invitation might have you dining on some strange local delicacies. Be brave though, if it's cooked it means it's already dead and can't bite!

Music is a universal language

If you have an interest in music, regardless of type, why not join a concert club, or musical appreciation society? If there isn't one locally, you could always start one.

Listen, dare and do

Listen out for new words and dare yourself to use them in conversation. It's only by taking part in ordinary everyday activities that you will increase your vocabulary. Making mistakes is all part of using a new language and no one is going to look down on you for trying.

Find a way to incorporate your new words into the activities you enjoy. Learn all the verbs associated with your chosen sport or hobby – and get out there and use them.

Getting to know you

Most of the tips in this section are to show you ways of getting to know people and integrating as quickly as possible. The only way to get over homesickness, and that feeling of not quite fitting in, is to meet people, let them get to know you, make new friends, and actively enjoy your new life.

Expat trivia

The Office for National Statistics said long-term migration from the UK reached 385,000 in the year to July 2006, the highest figure since current counting methods were introduced in 1991.

Summary

- If possible, learn the language before you arrive.

- Join a club or association to integrate faster.

- Ask the local council if language lessons are available for immigrants.

- Cultivate an interest in your local community – volunteer for something.

- Watch the commercials to pick up current usage of words.

- Quiz programmes with questions on screen help to increase vocabulary.

- Read children's books or magazines with lots of pictures.

- Take classes (such as dancing) to learn new skills.

- Listen out for new words and find ways to use them.

- Expect to be homesick – it's a normal reaction to moving country.

- Make a list of why you moved countries to look at when feeling homesick.

- Keep in touch with family and friends by phone, email and instant messaging.

- Shopping in smaller outlets gives you the opportunity to practise the language.

- Search online for goods from home you cannot do without.

- Buy a cookery book to learn about the local dishes.

HOUSES
FOR
SALE

Castles in the air

chapter 5
Castles in the air

It is amazing how otherwise sensible people leave their commonsense at home when buying property abroad. Don't join the 'wish I hadn't done that' club! Stop and think before signing for that too good to be true bargain. Running water and electricity really are essential, even (or especially) when the estate agent assures you that he and his family have lived without them for generations.

Rent a while

Before committing yourself to a property, or even an area, it is a good idea to rent. But what questions should you be asking?

- What is the minimum length of a long-term lease? In some countries there is a cut-off point whereby if you want to rent for longer than six months you find yourself tied in for three years.

- What are the hidden costs of renting? Often there is a finder's fee to be paid to the agent. This can be two months rent, or even more.

- What legal documents need to be provided? This varies considerably from country to country, so do ask before signing a lease. You might only need to show your passport, or you could have to produce proof of income and loads of paperwork proving you are who you claim to be.

Seasoning the mix

Let's say you've seen the ideal area and can't wait to start house hunting in earnest, is now the time to scour estate agents' windows for that perfect property? The answer should only be yes if you have visited or stayed there over more than one season. The tranquil fishing village that appears so romantic in autumn could be a tourist trap during the summer with hordes of rowdy visitors making the residents' lives a misery. Or the beauty spot, so idyllic in summer, might be completely isolated during long and lonely winter months. Don't allow estate agents to convince you all is well, regardless of how helpful they appear to be. Mistakes in choosing the area could sour your attitude to the new country as a whole.

City, town or country and other factors

Have a clear idea of what you want long before you go anywhere near an estate agent. Make a list of the things that are important, those you could never compromise on, and a second list of 'nice to haves' which you can take or leave.

The price is right

When hunting for property, shop around. Very often the same house will be on sale with different agencies and the price can differ by quite astounding amounts. In areas where there is a high percentage of expats, local agencies are often cheaper than those where English is spoken. It's worth doing a fair amount of window shopping and price comparison before viewing.

Where have all the houses gone?

If, like most people, you've done some property searching online and have arrived with a list of properties you'd like to view, don't be surprised when you are told they were all sold yesterday.

Many properties, particularly the attractive ones, are left online for months after they have been sold. The price shown may not reflect the current market trends, either. Expect prices to be higher than those on the Internet, that way you can be pleasantly surprised if they aren't.

Fees, quirks and local charges

Imagine you've found the house of your dreams, calculated your finances and discovered you can afford to go ahead. You sign on the dotted line and only then discover all the charges that go on top of the price shown in the agent's window. The extras can add a hefty percentage to the overall cost – to the extent that the house you loved could easily become the property you hate because it has put you in debt.

Don't forget to add on the cost of anything you will need to do to make the house a home. Whether it's a new shower, having fly screens fitted, security fencing erected, or air-conditioning installed. If it is something that has to be done straight away, the cost should be factored into your equation.

The house itself is in debt

In some countries outstanding debts are sold with the property. So if the current owner hasn't paid the telephone bill, or is behind on the rates, the new owner could end up as liable for the debt. If that is the law in your new country, get your solicitor to check the house isn't in debt before you sign for it.

Um, we seem to have two houses

Don't sign for a property unless you are in a position to go ahead with the purchase. If the sale of your current home has not gone through, don't assume all will be well. You could find yourself with a house you cannot sell in one country and a house in another that you cannot afford to buy.

Apart from the financial burden this brings, the stress factor of trying to juggle finances so that you don't lose deposits and other associated costs is not something you need when you have just moved country, or are in the process of doing so.

Buddy, can you spare a dime?

Mortgages may not be available until you are officially resident, or you might find you are only able to borrow a lower percentage if you are classed as non-resident. If you need to borrow money to purchase a house, and you are not able to secure the loan you need in your new country, don't give up hope. It is worth asking your bank in your home country, or checking with financial institutes in off-shore centres.

But, as has already been stated, don't sign for the new house until the finance is in place!

Survey, what survey?

Regardless of what may be the custom at home, in many countries no survey is carried out prior to purchase. For your own peace of mind, as well as avoiding what could turn out to be a costly mistake, arrange your own survey. Ask the estate agent for a list of surveyors. If the agency doesn't know of any, get onto the expat website for your country and area and ask for advice. You might be able to find an expat who is either still a practising surveyor, or who has retired but would be prepared to look over a property for you for a reasonable fee. The forum should be able to recommend a local surveyor.

Solicitations

Don't be surprised if the solicitor acting for the vendor turns out to be your solicitor as well. It is the custom, particularly in many European countries, for one solicitor to act for both purchaser and seller. It would be worthwhile employing your own independent solicitor. Although this will increase the cost of your purchase, being able to relax and sleep at night will be worth the extra money involved.

Utility check

Before signing on the bottom line, make sure you know all you need to about the utilities. Ask to see the bills for the last year. Find out about local taxes. Some countries have two annual taxes on property. One calculated on occupancy and the other on the rateable value of the actual property. Ask about mains sewage and how the cost is calculated. Is it a set rate, worked out on the usage of mains water, or metered separately?

On the same subject, ask if there is, in fact, mains sewage. Septic tanks are usually trouble-free, but you don't want to find yourself in the pooh, thinking everything flushed right away, only to discover it hasn't gone quite as far as you'd hoped.

Size matters

Oh yes, it does! Don't let anyone tell you differently. Property overseas is often much cheaper than in the home country, and suddenly the opportunity arises to purchase a ten-bedroom mansion abroad at the same price as the three-bedroom semi you've just sold. What a bargain, you think. Well, think again.

The financial cost of heating, cleaning and maintaining a much bigger home can be ruinous. As for all those extra rooms, do you really need them? Playing lord and lady of the newly acquired manor soon palls when it's time to redecorate, rewire or even re-roof a house three times bigger than you actually need.

Letting it out

You might find a property that suits you down to the ground, but which is too large. If it can be subdivided, it might be possible to let out part of the property for holiday rentals, or even a long-term rental, for some extra income. Before you get carried away with dreams of what you can spend the extra money on, you need to ask some searching questions.

- What would it cost to do the subdivision?
- How feasible would it be to let during the holiday season?
- What are the regulations covering holiday accommodation?
- What are the regulations covering long-term rentals?

- What would be the tax implications?

- What are the social implications of having strangers living so close?

- What would be your legal position if the tenant was unsatisfactory, but refused to leave?

The grass isn't just greener...

... there could be lots more of it. Even if the building isn't too large, don't be fooled into thinking owning acres of land is a step closer to the good life. All land requires care of some kind, whether it is mowing the grass or organising cattle or sheep to cut it for you.

Your land is my land

If you do arrange for a local farmer to graze his livestock on your land, or you buy a property where part of it is being used for that purpose, ask your solicitor to check whether you are at risk of losing the right to the land. In some countries, if land has been used unchallenged for a set period of time, the person using the land can lay claim to it – often without having to pay anything in exchange.

Rights of passage

Ask whether anyone has the right to cross your land – any part of it! I once viewed a property that was perfect in every way, except for the fact that half the town had the right to walk through the garden as a shortcut to the shops!

Smallholdings can mean large problems

If you have visions of living close to nature and being self-sufficient, do remember that the day will start early and finish late. Unless you have already run a smallholding you could be in for a rude awakening – and not just from the cock crowing in the middle of the night!

Read as much as you can, attend courses, visit smallholding associations and take off the rose-tinted spectacles. Running a successful smallholding could be harder work for less reward than you might imagine.

Off the beaten track

Peace, tranquillity and nature – what could be better? Well, a few shops so that you can buy milk, bread and other perishable essentials would be an asset. Being off the beaten track is great, just as long as you don't feel isolated.

New build

In some countries the building regulations may be more lax than you are used to, but that doesn't mean you should go with the flow. The number of programmes showing expats who have lost their life savings should be warning enough, but just in case it isn't, here are some things to watch out for if you go down the route of buying off-plan.

- Make sure the land is owned by the developer.

- Ask for proof of his building licence.

- Check that the land has permission for the type of development and dwellings envisaged.

- Get your solicitor to check that all legal requirements have been met.

- Insist on a builder's surety bond or guarantee to protect your investment.

- Only pay for work completed, do not be coerced into paying upfront for building works.

- Insist on a penalty clause for late completion.

Community living

Buying on a complex and gaining the benefits of community assets, such as swimming pools, tennis courts and gardens, could be the answer if you want all those things, but are not in a financial position to have them all.

Do bear in mind that maintenance of lifts, hallways, passageways and roads, in fact any communal area including the recreational ones mentioned above, as well as water and electricity costs relating to them, are shared by the community. This usually takes the form of an annual or monthly levy. Always ask about levies when viewing properties on a shared complex.

Ruined dreams

The idea of renovating a ruin, or upgrading an old property to modern standards, is something that many expats find appealing. And so it is; my husband and I have gone down that route ourselves many times. The downside is the cost factor. Unless you keep a tight rein on the purse strings, your dream of renovating a ruin could turn into a nightmare.

- Before committing yourself, get quotes for everything from the roof down to the garden gate.

- Whatever the total comes to, add on at least another twenty-five percent.

- Have a pest control expert examine the place for signs of termite, beetle or other infestations.

- Ask around and find a local builder who is prepared to introduce you to other satisfied customers – preferably a builder who understands English, unless your language skills are first-rate.

- Find out what the property would be worth once renovated – if it is considerably below the total you would have to pay to purchase and have the work done, then think very carefully before going ahead with it.

In the swim

If you have never had a swimming pool to maintain, but intend to have one in your new home, read as much as you can about pool maintenance before installing one, or buying a home with a pool already installed. Paying someone to come in regularly to look after the pool could be a major expense and not following the rules of water and hygiene controls might mean you end up feeling blue when the water goes green.

Resale reality

Are you are thinking in terms of a quick resale and moving on to the next property? Then you should think long and hard before you buy the first one. Housing markets in many countries are relatively stable. Very often the local populace buy or rent a property for life, so there may not be a resale market for your home.

Lock up

If you intend spending time travelling, either to see more of your new country or the world at large, do bear in mind the security aspect of leaving your home uninhabited. Look for a smaller property you can leave securely locked up. And, while we're on the subject of locks...

Lock down

Whatever and wherever you buy, one thing to do as soon as the property is yours is to have all the locks changed. The estate agent may be honest, but who is to say how many copies have been made of the keys while the house has been on the market? Or, in the case of a new-build, can you trust everyone who worked on the property and had access to the keys?

Expat trivia

An estimated 5.5m British people live permanently overseas — very nearly one in ten of the present population. Two-thirds of those emigrated to seek employment in a new country.

Summary

- If possible rent for a while before buying a property.

- If you cannot rent then visit over various seasons.

- House prices can vary from agent to agent – so window shop.

- Use the Internet as a guide only, as property is often more expensive.

- The all-in cost can be significantly higher than expected.

- Is the house in debt? In some countries you buy the debt with the property.

- Mortgages may not be available or have onerous conditions.

- Surveys are not standard in many countries and you may need to insist on one.

- Check the costs of utilities – and make sure they exist.

- Your land rights can slip if you allow continual usage.

- Peace and tranquillity is great, but don't live too far from shops for essentials.

- New build properties can be problematic. Have a solicitor look at all the issues.

- Living on a complex has benefits, but also many neighbours.

- Doing up a ruin is fun, but it is also hard work and can present problems.

- Check the realities of resale of property before you buy.

Making the connections

chapter 6
Making the connections

Technology is something we tend to take for granted, so it can come as a shock to find that not all countries make the right connections. From trains and boats and planes to electronic communication, knowing about potential problems makes it easier to deal with them, if and when they arise.

Letters pray

Home postal deliveries are not standard throughout the world. Some countries do not operate a delivery service in every town. If you are intending to work from home and regular mail deliveries are vital, or if that weekly letter from your sister is essential to your wellbeing, it is important to establish how reliable the postal service is. This is one of the areas where a visit to an online forum is a must. Ask expats who live in the region what the postal system is like. Post office boxes and courier service may be the way you need to go. Regardless of what estate agents and other interested bodies tell you, the post doesn't always get through.

Mail forwarding

Even if your chosen location has wonderful mail deliveries, you might still find it helpful to subscribe to a mail forwarding system (e.g. **www.my-uk-mail.co.uk**) whereby you have a street address in your home country to receive mail.

This can be very useful when:

- You want to buy something online, but the retailer won't ship the goods overseas.

- Or the shipping costs are very high and the purchase carries additional charges.

- The retailer won't accept an overseas address for credit card payments.

The way the system works is that you are notified when you receive mail in your country of origin. The mail is then consolidated into one package, saving you money on shipping costs. You stipulate how often you want your mail and/ or parcels delivered to you, and how you would like them delivered – by courier or normal mail.

If you are waiting for important documents these can be scanned and emailed to you.

There are many of these mail forwarding companies, so it pays to shop around before you leave.

International email addresses

Until such time as you have your own home set up as you would like, the chances are you won't be able to get a local email address. Before leaving your home country make sure you sign up to one of the free email addresses, such as Hotmail, and give that address to everyone who matters to you. That way you can check your emails and keep family and friends up to date on your new life at any cybercafé.

Computer to computer talking

The cost of phoning the loved ones left behind can be prohibitive, but there are ways of staying in touch free of charge. As long as you have an Internet connection you can use the computer as a telephone. There are various free programmes to download which offer Internet telephony. Provided the person you wish to speak to has the same programme (or one that is compatible) you can chat all day free of charge.

One of the easiest to install and use is Skype: **www.skype.com**

Other good services to investigate:

Delta Three: **www.deltathree.com**

Net2Phone: **www.net2phone.com**

Vonage: **www.vonage.com**

Computerised calls out

Some of the above programmes offer a 'call out' service whereby you deposit an amount with them and then use your computer as a normal phone, calling all over the world cheaper than using a standard service. This means that even if Great Aunt Alice hasn't yet made it to the electronic age, you can still use your computer to call her home phone at a much lower rate than standard telephone charges.

Computerised calls in

Skype offers a service whereby you can purchase a telephone number in your home country. The cost is minimal and the benefits to people who call you regularly are amazing.

Let's say you move to Australia from the UK, the cost of international telephone calls could prevent your family left behind from keeping regular contact. But with Skype's system you buy a UK telephone number, so that anyone calling you will be charged national (or local) and not international rates.

So, whether you relocate to Argentina, Austria or Algeria (or a country starting with any other letter of the alphabet) you can take a UK number with you.

Internet or internot?

Depending on where you end up in the world, connecting to the World Wide Web may not be as easy as calling up a local service provider and asking for the latest broadband package. Even being in a first world country doesn't guarantee an Internet connection. In Spain, for example, in areas where the infrastructure hasn't yet caught up with the population explosion, it can be quite difficult to get regular telephone and broadband coverage.

If you find your little corner of the globe doesn't yet have the facilities you need, fear not. There are ways to overcome the problem by hooking up to a satellite connection.

The following offer satellite services:

www.primesatellitebroadband.com/internetaccess.htm

www.directglobal.net/satellite_broadband_internet.htm

www.spidersat.net

www.bcsatellite.net

www.internet-satellite-access-connection.co.uk

www.diacomm.net

www.satsig.net

It's been good to see you

As has already been mentioned, staying in touch with those you leave behind can help you to deal with homesickness. The feeling of being cut off from loved ones is one of the reasons so many struggle with living abroad.

A great way to circumvent this, once you've sorted out your Internet connection, is to make use of a webcam. Set one up on your computer and, each time you chat using the online telephone services, your friends and family can see you. At the same time, providing you've stressed to them the importance of having a webcam, you can see them on your computer screen. It's almost like having visitors in your home, only you don't need to bake a cake!

Tippy, tappy talking

Another way to maintain regular contact, without it costing anything at all, is to chat using an online messenger service, such as Microsoft's MSN.

Go to **www.msn.com or www.msn.co.uk** to download
the software. The beauty of that kind of contact is that
several people can 'talk' by typing at the same time in the
same window.

Once again, having a webcam set up means you can see and/or
be seen if you choose.

Put a socket in it

If you are taking electronic equipment, such as multimedia,
printer and computer, you will most probably have to change
all the plugs when you set up your system. To save having to do
that immediately, it's a good idea to invest in some multipoint
sockets to take with you. This means you only need to change
the plug on the multipoint instead of on each individual item.

Power surge alert

Because electrical storms and variable power supply problems
are common in many overseas countries—which can cause
equipment damage—it's a good idea to make sure the
multipoint sockets are power surge protected.

Distance is relative

When you look for somewhere to settle, do bear in mind you
might want to have a relatively easy route to an airport. If you
are going to have family and friends coming to visit your new
home the chances are you'll be picking them up. Travelling
several hours each way once a year is one thing, but if you have
a stream of visitors during the course of the year, that can get
extremely wearing.

Or boats and trains

Think ahead about the kind of transport system that will make keeping in touch with the folks back home as convenient as possible. If, for example, you have moved to Europe from the UK, you could make life easier for yourself, and future visitors, by looking into the transport options available to you. Mainline train stations that connect with the Eurostar line, or easy access to a ferry port, would make it feel less final when you cross the channel.

A bus, a bus, my kingdom for a bus

Look carefully at the local public transport options. In some countries these can range from dreadful to dangerous. A bus ride on the island of Gozo remains memorable because everyone began praying as soon as the bus moved; only stopping when the bus did.

Whatever the weather

Before you settle down to life on an island which appears to have excellent ferry and/or helicopter connections with the mainland, make enquiries about what happens during peak tourist times, or when the weather is too bad for the ferry to run.

Spring and autumn might be trouble-free, but you could find yourself stranded without a ferry service during periods of poor weather in winter, or face dreary hours in a queue for the ferry during the summer when hordes of tourists flock to the island.

Summary

- In many countries it will be necessary to set up a post office box in the nearest town.

- Use mail-forwarding services in the UK for those items you buy online but cannot have shipped to your new country.

- Internet telephony is the cheapest way to stay in touch. It's free even if you talk all day long! If you add a webcam you can even have face to face conversations.

- Setting up a UK number through the service means everyone can call you anywhere in the world at local rates.

- Internet services vary from country to country. If you find yourself in an area without easy access to broadband it is worth looking at satellite as an alternative. There are a number of options available.

- If you are unable to source plugs for all your essential appliances, such as computer and printer, then buy a number of multipoint adapters to take with you. Make sure your appliances comply with the voltage in the new country.

- Many countries, and not only in the third world, have massive power fluctuations so it is essential to attach power surge protected plugs and multipoint adapters as a priority.

- Find out how easy it is to access trains and boat and planes if you will have regular visitors, or if you need to travel on business.

Plan to work

chapter 7
Plan to work

Taking up the challenge of a new job abroad, or starting a
business in a foreign environment, takes some careful planning.
The following tips should help you to avoid the snares lying in
wait for the unwary.

Snakes and ladders

Not all countries accept qualifications on a like for like basis.
Before planning your great escape to a new life overseas it is
important to find out how your qualifications equate in your
chosen country. You might be pleasantly surprised and find
you have jumped a few rungs on the business hierarchy ladder,
but you might also have slid down the odd snake and have to
accept a lowlier position.

I'll do anything for you, dear

Sometimes, in our desire to change our lives, we make rash
decisions that can have devastating effects. It is possible to
take up new challenges, such as a change of career into a new
and untried direction, but do make sure you want to do the job
on offer. Taking on a job that is going to make you miserable,
just to get a work permit, isn't worth the anguish. You might
think you can stand it for a couple of years, but if you hate
going to work every day, those two years will feel like eternity.

Working in a foreign language

Having a second language adds enormously to your employability factor, particularly if it's the language of the country you are moving to. But even if it isn't, multinational companies are always on the lookout for linguists, so if you studied a second language at school, even if you haven't used it for decades, it might be a good idea to bring it up to speed before applying for a job overseas.

How important is job security to you?

Thousands of people move abroad without a fixed job offer and make a go of it, but there are thousand of others who fail to find regular work. If you are the type of person who needs the security of a fixed pay check, standard hours and company benefits, then don't even think of leaving the country until you have found the perfect job – and even then you'll need to bear in mind that things can go wrong.

Same company, new country

Before you give up your current employment to seek pastures new, why not ask if you can work from home? In these days of telecommuting it doesn't really matter where you are in the world, other than taking time differences into account for conference calls and the like. You might find your employers would rather keep you on with electronic contact than lose you altogether.

Hey, I'm unique!

Try to find out if you have a particular skill that isn't common in the country you want to live in. Anything that makes your CV stand out (in a good way, of course) should have pride of place near the top where it will be noticed.

It's your business to find out

Okay, so you've received a fantastic job offer. You can't believe your luck! Actually, if the offer is that fantastic, rather than believe your luck, it might be better to do some research and make sure it is real.

Ask questions, not just of your future employers, but anyone and everyone who can tell you something about the company. If the job isn't with a multi-national conglomerate you should think about running a check on the company and directors. You don't want to find out, shortly after relocating, that the company you have based your move on is heading for liquidation.

Can you speak to an employee?

Ask if you can be put in touch with other employees. This isn't just to reassure yourself that the company is sound, although it will help to do so. Chatting to your future workmates before you arrive by phone, email or messenger, means you won't feel so much like a new kid at school on your first day at work.

Workaday ins and outs

Do remember that employment conditions, such as hours, working week, holiday entitlement, pension, health benefits, taxation levels, and dismissal notice periods vary from country to country. Make sure all of these important issues are covered in your contract or letter of employment.

Commuter blues

Ask about the housing situation in the area. If you are moving to a university town you need to know, even if your employment has nothing whatsoever to do with the university. Accommodation to rent and property to buy is usually scarce in such towns and could mean you have to live far from your place of employment, leading to lengthy commutes each morning and evening. Alternatively, if you want to live in the town, you might be charged a very high rental or have to pay far more for a house than you had budgeted for.

Can the salary cope with the local cost of living?

Do your homework on cost of living compared with your new salary. Earning three million 'whatevers' a year is only brilliant if you can live on less than that. On the other hand, you might take a pay cut and yet have a better standard of living than you do now. If you aren't able to make contact with other company employees, try the expat forums to get an idea of what sort of wage would be needed to live comfortably.

Promotion and salary increases?

What are the prospects regarding promotion and salary increase? Don't be afraid to rock the boat by asking before you sign a contract or organise your removals. If you are nervous about raising the subject before you leave, in case they don't give you the job, imagine how much less likely you are to ask for a pay increase once you are in the new country and staying there is dependent on keeping your job.

Contractually speaking

No matter how good the offer, no matter how great the life sounds, don't commit yourself without getting a signed contract. But remember, just having a contract doesn't mean you should jump on the next plane – have the contract vetted before you sign it. Make a list of all the things that are important to you and make sure they are all covered to your satisfaction.

I'm going to be paid in what?

If the country has a weak or a fluctuating economy try to negotiate having your salary paid in a strong internationally accepted currency. It's all very well living in paradise, but if your super salary is only worth two coconuts and a hand of bananas by the time you draw it out of the bank, paradise isn't going to seem quite so attractive.

But it's my money!

Some countries have exchange control mechanisms in place that would shame the guardians of Fort Knox. You may live in your new home for the rest of your life without wanting to transfer any money out, but you need to know that you can do so if a need arises.

Daylight come and I wanna go home

Find out what penalties (if any) you might have to pay if you want to break your contract because you and your new employer don't hit it off, or homesickness becomes too much to bear. If at all possible, put a small nest egg to one side before you move country, so that you are not completely tied into a company.

Permit me to tell you

Find out from the Department of Employment's website in your new country what the situation is regarding your work permit if your contract expires. Are you free to find another job using the existing permit, or would you have to apply for another one? By all means ask your prospective employer, but don't just take their word for it. There are many unscrupulous employers who will tell you exactly what you want to hear – not what you need to know.

Permitted to know

Getting a permit to work can be the easiest thing in the world to sort out, or it can be a nightmare of expensive red tape, with every piece of paper having some sort of fee attached. Ask your prospective employer who deals with arranging the work permit, and who pays the costs. If getting the permit is down to you, ask the company to put you in touch with the right people.

If they say they don't know who to go to, or where to start, you should think twice before working for them. If they regularly recruit overseas staff they should know the answers to your questions.

Check entry dates for work permit

When the permit arrives check it carefully to see if there are any dates by which you have to arrive in the country, or a date before which you shouldn't land. There is often a window of a few weeks during which time the permit has to be validated. Imagine going to all that trouble of organising the move and then, because you get there on the wrong day, you are refused entry! I shouldn't think you'd be at the top of your family's Christmas card list, would you?

One permit, how many can work?

You can't take it for granted that because one of you has a work permit the spouse will be able to find a job as well. Often a work permit is only for the breadwinner and the spouse would have to apply for a separate permit if he or she wishes to work.

Don't pay to try to get paid

There are many reputable employment agencies recruiting staff to work overseas, but there are also some sharks. If an agency asks you to pay an upfront fee before they will try to find you a job, take your request elsewhere. The agency should be paid by the employer for finding them the right employee. If an agency is making money from the signing on fees, the incentive to find you work isn't there.

A ticket to ride?

If you are only intending to live abroad for the duration of a work contract, have you made sure you could afford to return home at the end of the period? Some employers offer a ticket home as part of the package, but what if they don't keep to their word? If it isn't in the contract you may have difficulty getting them to pay.

Don't forget the paperwork

Make photocopies of all your work-related papers and have them notarised before you move abroad. Don't hand over any original documents or certificates — just in case they go missing. Make sure you have at least one other copy (as well as the original) of anything that you give to your new employers. The reason for this is simple, if things don't work out and you want to change jobs, you need to be able to supply your credentials without worrying about trying to get original documents back from your existing employer.

Have CV will update

Keep your CV on disk and/or home computer so that you can update it, print out a new copy, or email it as an attachment to a prospective employer.

Running a business or a business running you?

The number of people who decide to throw everything up and move abroad to run a bar, café, hotel, painting and decorating concern, taxi service or any other kind of business without any experience is staggering. Don't join them! Most of these people either go to the wall in the first year or spend many years in absolute misery while they learn everything they should have found out before moving abroad. If it's hard to take on a new business without experience in your home country, it is several times harder in a foreign country. If you really want to run a tearoom in Outer Mongolia, then learn how to do it in your home country first. It will still be difficult in your new country, but at least you'll have some idea of how to succeed.

Time off – what's that?

Before you sink your life savings into that seaside bar and restaurant, ask yourself if you really want to work seven days a week, with longer hours each day than you've ever worked before. Any business in a tourist region tends to be seasonal. If the season is short you will need to earn enough during that period to support you for the entire year. Time off could become a treasured, but almost forgotten, memory.

Me, myself, I, alone – I hope!

Some countries operate a protectionist system whereby you have to have a local partner to open a business. Other countries are even more stringent in that you would be allowed to own a business, but not work in it yourself. A good example of this would be someone owning a hotel, but not being allowed to answer the telephone or take bookings.

Generally these rules are in place to generate local employment and protect local businesses from being taken over by outsiders. If you want to make sure you can work in your own business, or be allowed to run it without taking on a partner you don't need or want, you should ask the local Chamber of Commerce what the regulations are.

Tangled up in red tape

If you fret and fume because of the bureaucracy of your local council, then running your own business abroad is most probably not going to do your blood pressure any good. Some countries have so much red tape they could use it to gift-wrap the world. Regulations you cannot even begin to imagine will rule your every waking moment. If this is your idea of hell, then running your own business abroad is possibly not for you – unless you can dump all the bureaucracy on your more patient spouse.

Contact the local Chamber of Commerce

To avoid the stress of finding out too late that your chosen country is one of the red tape brigade, it's a good idea to contact the Chamber of Commerce where you want to settle. Ask what the regulations are for setting up your own business. What papers will you need? Would you need to provide a deposit to be held as security against insolvency? Are there any associations you would have to join? Any credentials you would have to prove? Some businesses without regulatory bodies in one country can have very strict controls in another.

Making sure of your market

To save yourself both heartache and wallet ache it is essential you do your homework and establish whether there is a need for your type of business in the area you want to settle. Wishing and hoping is not going to provide customers, and without people to pay you, you'll soon be in trouble.

Try to find out if someone else has tried your idea and failed. If they have, and you can establish what mistakes were made, you might be able to succeed, but keep grounded in reality – did they fail because of mistakes, or because there wasn't a market?

Find a legal eagle

Setting up a new business abroad without knowing the legalities is like entering a marathon when the furthest you've ever run is to the local bus stop. Whatever the business, large or small, existing or start-up, the rules, laws and regulations will defeat you without having someone on your side who can speak the language, understand the paperwork and guide you through the maze of bureaucracy. Don't try to fly on your own – employ a legal eagle.

Another good reason for employing someone local to help you set up your business is that they will be aware of all the tax breaks available.

Buying an existing business

Owning a business in which you do not hold a qualification is not allowed in some countries. So, if you have a yearning to own a hairdressing salon, or some other enterprise requiring recognised qualifications, and thought that all you needed to do was employ qualified staff, you should check the regulations through the Chamber of Commerce before signing on the dotted line.

Beware of friendly fire

Just because the person selling the business is from your home country, or even your home town, does not mean he or she is automatically trustworthy. More expats get their fingers burnt by their fellow countrymen than they do by the locals. Keep a healthy scepticism and ask to see all the paperwork – and then ask your legal eagle and accountant to go through the books.

Expat trivia

Of the 2.5 million British expats worldwide who are still eligible to vote in UK General and European elections only 20,000 registered to vote in the UK in 2005.

Staff and a half

Before taking on any staff you should find out what your contribution would be towards their social security cost. In some countries the employer's contribution is a crippling percentage of the total wage bill. If you buy an existing business and you want to dismiss the staff because they are inefficient, or you simply don't want to have employees, you should find out (again before buying the business) what the legal situation is. You might find yourself saddled with several employees who do nothing, while you and your family work yourselves to a frazzle, and yet you cannot fire them.

Selling up and selling on

There may well come a time when you have had enough of working and want to retire. That is not the time to find out that no one wants to take your business on, or, if they do, are not prepared to pay a fair price for it. This could happen if you started a new business from scratch and, when you come to sell, there is no one qualified to take over. Thinking ahead is essential. You need to be as certain as you can be that you'll be able to recoup your capital when the time comes. One way to ensure this is to train your staff so that prospective purchasers aren't put off by lack of continuity in management.

Summary

- Check to see that your qualifications will be honoured.

- Are your linguistic skills up to the task of working in a foreign language?

- Remember there is no such thing as job security, so have contingency plans.

- Can you stay with your present employer, but work abroad?

- Before taking the job research the company thoroughly.

- Find out about holidays, pension, health benefits and tax.

- Don't move abroad without a written contract.

- Who arranges the work permit and how many can work?

- What happens if you leave before the contract expires?

- Is there housing near to work or will you be faced with a long commute?

- Is the salary high enough to cope with the cost of living?

- If a ticket home is part of the job offer make sure it says so in the contract.

- Don't run a business abroad that you haven't run at home.

- Get legal advice before buying an existing business or starting a new one.

- Find out about staff social security payments.

Choose to play

chapter 8
Making a difference

A full and active lifestyle suited to your particular needs will ensure you settle easily in your new home, but have you considered all the ramifications of how to attain that blissful state? Retirement might not be the ideal relaxing situation you had envisioned. As with every other aspect of moving abroad, the more groundwork you do before you leave home, the better your chances of being one of those who are happy in their new country.

Avoid those retirement blues

Imagine life as one long holiday, day after day relaxing by the pool, eating, drinking, sleeping and doing little else. It may sound heavenly, and for a few months it might even feel that way, but boredom will set in sooner or later. Before that happens, why not make a list of everything you can think of that has ever interested you? You'll be amazed at the things you've forgotten you were passionate about.

An interest in horses could lead to a part time job in the local stables. Or a love of old buildings could develop into working as a local tour guide a few hours a week during the season. Think laterally and reawaken all those dormant interests.

Volunteer

If time is hanging heavy on your hands and you'd like to put something into your local community, or even do something for a nationwide charity, why not contact the British Council, or charities with international units? Another good starting point would be contacting Voluntary Services Overseas. The VSO tries to match people's skills and professional background with the need for volunteers ranging in age from 17 to 75:

http://www.vso.org.uk/

Take up a new sport or hobby

Tennis, golf and bowls (or local versions of bowls such as pétanque in France) are all sports that you could take up, but how about really taking the plunge and learning to snorkel or scuba dive? Why not get over your hang ups and hang-glide? Drop your inhibitions, your body and possibly your sanity, too, and join a parachute club.

A degree of knowledge

Wake up the grey matter to some degree by taking a correspondence course. The choices are boundless — from joining Open University to taking a flour-milling correspondence training programme through the National Association of British and Irish Millers (always assuming you've bought a mill). The only limit is one you impose on your imagination and time. If "a little learning is a dangerous thing", just think how much fun you could have with a lot!

A wise man will make more opportunities than he finds.

Sir Francis Bacon (1561 - 1626)

Learn a foreign language

If you are moving to a country where the home language is not English, then this is one you should do as a matter of course to help you integrate. But even if you go to an English-speaking country, learning a new language can be both fun and challenging. Pick your next holiday destination and aim to dazzle the locals with your linguistic skills.

The write thing to do

Do you remember the desire to be a steam train driver that absorbed you throughout your childhood? Or the adventurer in you who wanted to climb Everest? Now might be the time to return to your childhood dreams and turn them into a novel.

It's a family affair

You could write up your family tree, or at least the branches of it that interest you. Lots of information is available online and a copy of *The Greatest Genealogy Tips in the World* by Maureen Vincent-Northam will point you in the right direction.

Become a traveller

If your finances stretch that far you could buy a camper van and stretch your horizons as well. One of the delights of moving abroad is seeing the country and it's much easier to cover ground if you aren't tied to hotels and fixed itineraries.

Become snap happy

Photography is a wonderful hobby, combining both artistic ability and expression. It has never been easier to take great pictures than it is in today's digital world. If there isn't a camera club in your area, or if there is and you fear the language difficulties might be too great to overcome, there are online clubs to join. You never know, you might find your next door neighbour but one is an expat amateur photographer and you would never have met if you hadn't joined a camera club.

Painting for pleasure

Most people say they can't draw or paint, but many of us have never actually tried. You might find the inspiration of living in your new surroundings enough to make you reach for pad and brushes.

And if it turns out you have ability, you might try selling a few of your masterpieces at the local market, which is another good way of getting to know a few more of the local residents.

Get in on the act

Why not join the local amateur dramatics society? Even if your language skills aren't enough to get you up on the stage, most societies are short of workers to paint scenery, shift sets, make costumes, sell tickets and one hundred and one other jobs that have to be tackled so that the show can go on.

Crossing words

Do you have a large vocabulary and an interest in puzzles? Many newspapers and magazines need crosswords or other brainteasers for their entertainment pages. There are several books available to teach you how to compile crosswords and other puzzles. As a hobby it is mentally stimulating – and you can earn some extra spending money as well!

Talking, talking, talking, happy talk

Teaching English as a foreign language (TEFL) is an option you might want to think about. Courses are available as distance learning online, or you could attend a course before you leave home, so that you are ready to take on students as soon as you've settled into your new country.

Get fit and keep fit

The fitter and more active you are, the more pleasure you'll get from your retirement. Learning exercises in a foreign language can be hilarious. You might find yourself bobbing up as the rest of the class ducks down, but don't worry, you'll soon get to understand the actions, if not the words. If there isn't a keep fit class in the area, or this doesn't appeal to you, why not join (or start) a walking group? These are usually advertised in local papers.

Do things together

Building shared interests in something neither of you has ever done before will give you additional topics of conversation and the enjoyment of practising your new skill or sport as a couple. It could also mean meeting new people together, so that you can develop your social circle.

… and also on your own

One of the major problems when retiring is suddenly spending all day, every day, in each other's company. This is problematic enough when you are in a country you know, surrounded by family and friends and with outside interests. But if you take into account the unfamiliarity of living abroad and all the stress that entails, you'll be tearing each other to pieces if you don't develop some separate interests. Absence makes the heart grow fonder, and claustrophobic co-habitation can breed axe murderers.

Healthy and happy

As you will have noticed, most of the tips in this chapter are urging you to get out and do things. The reason for that is that it is easier for people to feel homesick and unhappy if they are bored. Taking up just one of the hobbies would mean that, at the very least, you'll get to know some new people. You could also get fit, learn a new skill and, most important of all, enjoy your new life.

Summary

- Join the Voluntary Service Overseas or find out from your local council where they need voluntary helpers.

- Take up a new hobby or sport. Nothing is more exhilarating than conquering a previously untried activity.

- Even if the new country is predominately English speaking why not tackle a new language for the sheer pleasure of it?

- Why not write a novel or your memoirs? Take a correspondence course, such as with Writers Bureau.

- Plot your family tree and find out where you and your family come from. You can do it from anywhere in the world!

- If you enjoy taking snaps, why not take a course or join a photography club?

- Learn to paint! If you are unable to find a local teacher why not search on the Internet for advice?

- Join an amateur dramatic society. Why not advertise in the local paper and start an English group?

- Teach English as a foreign language with TEFL or a similar course. It is also a way of bringing in additional income.

- Join a gym or exercise class. This gets you out of the house, keeps you fit, and also helps you to meet new people.

- Take up a new interest that both of you can enjoy. Try to choose something that is new to both of you.

- Don't spend all day every day in each other's pockets!

Highways & byways

chapter 9
Highways & byways

If you want to avoid being driven to drink, it's a good idea to do a little research about the dos and don'ts of the road ahead. From car registration to the overseas version of the MOT, you'll need to be prepared, to avoid hitting a wall of bureaucracy.

Have car, will travel?

If you are not taking your car with you, arrange for a service and advertise it for sale. You might be able to coordinate handover the day or so before you leave, but it is more likely the new owner will want to take possession as soon as possible, so you need to think about transport once the car has gone.

Insuring a safe journey

If your car is going to the new destination in the container, ask your shipping agent to arrange suitable insurance so that it can be driven from the moment it leaves the container.

If you are driving the car from your current country of residence to your new home, remember to contact your insurance company and make sure you are covered. Sometimes no longer being resident in your home country invalidates any existing insurance and you may need to re-insure shortly after arriving abroad. Also, because some countries do not recognise overseas insurers if you are taking up residence (as opposed to driving through the country on holiday) you may need to arrange new insurance before you go.

Car can go tango

Registering a car abroad can be a complex nightmare of red tape. Before you leave your home country it is essential that you have everything you might need to prove ownership and value of the vehicle. Make sure you have:

- The receipt to show how much you paid for the car.

- The log book, translated if necessary.

- Insurance papers.

- MOT certificate.

- Proof of identity (yours, not the car).

- Masses of patience.

- A cheque book with lots of cash available.

In most countries it is easier to buy a car and register it than re-register a foreign import.

Are EU legal?

Although the UK driving licence is classed as a European driving permit, taking up residence in a European country can require you to have your licence endorsed, or even exchanged for one issued by your new country's licensing authority. In most cases your UK licence is valid until you are officially resident. The following website defines normal residence and also lists the various authorities controlling licenses for European countries:

http://europa.eu.int/youreurope/nav/en/citizens/factsheets/eu/drivinglicence/overview/en.html

Trans-continental drift

It isn't only in Europe that the UK licence is recognised. Many countries throughout the world will allow you to exchange your UK (or US) driving licence for one issued by their own licensing authority, but in some cases this will still entail taking a written and/or practical test. Prior to receiving your new licence you may need to carry an International Driving Permit in addition to your normal driving licence. You will need to obtain this before leaving your home country as they cannot be issued retrospectively. Nor can they be issued more than three months in advance. To find out if your prospective new country requires an IDP visit the website of the AA or the RAC:

www.theaa.com

www.rac.co.uk

Information for American drivers wishing to drive abroad can be found at: **www.usa.gov**.

Be a learner driver – part one

As soon as possible after you arrive, or better still during one of your inspection visits, buy a copy of the Highway Code and (if needed) a dictionary to translate the terms. Don't assume the rules of the road are uniform across the world – you might find yourself breaking the law by doing what you thought was the right thing!

Be a learner driver – part two

Compare road signs in your Highway Code book at home with those in the new country's book. Make colour photocopies of any that differ and try to memorise the new ones.

Be prepared

You should find details in the Highway Code of what must be carried in the car at all times. If it isn't there, go on to one of the expat forums and ask, or visit the AA or RAC websites, as this is also something that varies from country to country.

In some countries you need a fire extinguisher and one triangle, in others, no fire extinguisher but two triangles and a first-aid kit. Do you need to keep your car papers with you at all times, or only your driving licence? Asking ahead of time could save embarrassing situations later.

Also, think about weather conditions and other environmental factors in your new country. For example, if you move to somewhere with harsh winters you might need to carry snow chains for the wheels. If you relocate to a country with poisonous spiders, snakes or scorpions, you may have to carry antidotes in the car.

Mobile phone rules, okay

Although you may see locals driving with one hand on the wheel and the other holding a mobile phone, it isn't safe to assume it's legal to do so. From the point of view of using a mobile phone in the car, a hands' free kit should keep you out of trouble with the local police force.

When you travel,
remember that a
foreign country is
not designed to make
you comfortable.
It is designed
to make its own
people comfortable.

Clifton Fadiman (1904 - 1999)

Child safety rules

Regulations about where a child can be in the car, and also what type of car seat is required may vary, but this information should be available from the Highway Code, which you will, by now, know off by heart and hate the sight of!

Are you permitted to drive here?

In countries where the original indigenous population have reserved land you might need special permits to drive across it. The expat forums for your new country will be able to answer this question and also tell you where to get a permit.

A moo-ving drive!

Watch out for livestock on the roads. Free range can mean exactly that in some countries. You might encounter large numbers of horse-drawn wagons carrying agricultural products on the public roads during harvest periods and, at night, unlit horse-drawn wagons can be a hazard.

Making sure left is right

If you are driving on the opposite side of the road for the first time, or it is many years since you last did so, it's a good idea to put something in the car to remind you which side of the road you should be on. In built up areas it won't be a problem, because the other road users will remind you, the danger will come on little-used roads when you turn left or right. If you don't have a sign on the dashboard, or something stuck on the appropriate side of the steering wheel, it is all too easy to forget – until you meet the vehicle coming straight at you!

I wasn't speeding, guv, honest!

Standard speed limits for different types of road vary from country to country. Trying to explain in Croatian that you thought you were obeying the speed limit is not how you want to practise your language skills.

Who moved the traffic lights?

If you come to a junction that you feel should have traffic lights (called robots in South Africa) and cannot see any, look up. Often the lights are suspended across the road. Check with the country's Highway Code to ensure you follow the signals; there may be minor differences in the way the amber light is used.

In case of emergency

Keep a list in the car of all the emergency numbers you might need. For example: police, fire, ambulance, roadside assistance and helicopter rescue (if driving on mountainous or remote roads).

It is also a good idea to memorise, as well as having a written translation, phrases you might need in an emergency. When your car is balanced on the edge of a precipice, and you are scared to breathe in case you tip it over, is not the time to start trying to learn a new language.

Be a shining light

It is essential to find out if car lights must be kept on in built up areas, even during daylight hours. Don't hide your light under a bushel – unless you can explain in creditable Foreign why you have done so.

Trams rule, okay?

In many countries trams are given priority at all times. You need to find out exactly when and how you are permitted to overtake them. For example, in Germany you can overtake trams on either side on one-way streets, but on a two-way street, it must be overtaken on the right. In most countries overtaking trams when their occupants are either climbing aboard or alighting is illegal.

Car wash capers

On the subject of Germany, it is illegal to wash your car in the street and you can be fined heavily for doing so. It is quite possible the same rule applies in other countries, so before you set to with bucket and sponge, ask your neighbours if it is legal.

Parking rights – and wrongs

Find out where and how you are allowed to park. In South Africa, for example, you must only park with your car facing the same direction as the flow of traffic. In Greece, if you park in a no parking zone or certain other areas, the police may remove your licence plates until you pay your traffic fine.

Isn't life a hoot?

Use of the horn is prohibited in built-up areas of many countries, except in cases of immediate and extreme danger, in other countries it's obligatory to use the horn to signal your intention to pass. The only way to know which type of country you are in is to ask.

Getting in a state

In certain countries made up of a federation of states or provinces, such as America or Australia, you might find that each state has different driving laws and regulations. If you intend to drive across several states it is essential to find out where the regulations differ.

Expat trivia

In the last survey taken (2006) Nigeria had the highest jump in expatriate retirees over the previous decade. The number choosing to relocate there rose by 667%.

Dry states and countries

Carrying alcohol across some 'dry' states in America or Islamic countries, even if the bottle is sealed and packed in the boot of the car, is against the law and can be punishable by imprisonment. This can be particularly problematic when travelling across the USA, where you might need to cross several state boundaries during the course of a journey. You might only want to take great-uncle Jim a Christmas gift of some dry sherry, but if it means spending the New Year in a cell, I should take him some nice socks instead!

Summary

- Ask your shipping agent to insure the car in transit.

- If driving have all the car's paperwork easily to hand.

- Research driving licence requirements before leaving the UK.

- Buy a copy of the local Highway Code so that you can know the regulations.

- Learn all the road signs so that they are instantly understood.

- Make sure the car is equipped to cover the country's accessory requirements.

- Do your child seats comply with all the regulations?

- Do you need a permit to cross any indigenous land?

- Put something in the car to remind you which side of the road to drive on.

- Keep a list of all the emergency numbers you might need in case of accident.

- Some countries have bizarre regulations, which are law.

- Parking rules and regulations vary from country to country.

- Don't hoot in built up areas unless you have checked it isn't against the law.

- Laws can vary from state to state in Australia and the USA.

- Don't carry alcohol across states or countries that are dry.

FIRST AID ⊞

EE

ASP

ANTISEPTIC

KNUCKLE BANDAGES AND
BUTTERFLY CLOSURES

NONASPIRIN

WOVEN ADHESIVE BANDAGES

PACK

INSECT STING
MEDICATION

The healthy options

chapter 10
The healthy options

Whether retiring or relocating to take up the challenge of a new job, your healthcare is something that needs to be considered long before you set out on your journey. Then, once you've arrived in your new country, there are ways of making sure your options are all healthy ones.

Check it out

Have a full medical before you leave, including (for lady readers) a mammogram and visit to a gynaecologist. Go to the dentist and have any necessary work done. If you wear glasses or contact lenses have an eye test and then...

I can see clearly now

Get a good supply of disposable contact lenses to see you through until you can register with an optician. Whether you wear contacts or glasses, ask your optician for a copy of your prescription. If your glasses break, or the contact lenses get lost, you should be able to arrange replacements quicker than if you had to organise an eye test first.

When the travelling stops, so does the cover

An important point to bear in mind is that travel insurance is no longer valid once you take up residence in a country. The cover isn't indefinite and is invalidated once you can no longer be regarded as travelling.

We're all Europeans now – aren't we?

A European Health Insurance Card (EHIC) entitles citizens of any European country to reduced-cost, sometimes free, medical treatment that becomes necessary whilst in a European Economic Area (EEA) country or Switzerland.

For information on obtaining a UK EHIC visit the Department of Health's website at: www.dh.gov.uk. Click on 'Policy and Guidance' then 'Advice for Travellers'.

You will most probably already have one of these cards if you have visited Europe since they were introduced in January 2006, but do remember, as with travel insurance, your card is no longer valid once you are permanently resident in another European country.

It will be necessary to contact the health authorities in your new country and request a new EHIC. This is particularly important if you intend to travel through Europe or return to the UK on vacation or for business.

Pensioner's Europe and beyond

If you are in receipt of a UK state pension you will be able to register with the healthcare authorities in any European country and receive the same healthcare benefits as the citizens of that country. This does not necessarily mean the healthcare is free, but the costs will certainly be less than paying for private health cover. To enable you to register it is necessary to apply for an E121 from the International Pension Service, **www.thepensionservice.gov.uk/ipc/home.asp**, which you present to the health authority in your new country.

Health is not valued till sickness comes.

Dr. Thomas Fuller (1654 - 1734), Gnomologia

If you are taking early retirement you can request form E106 which entitles you to state health care on the same basis as nationals of your new European country, but there are conditions attached. You are only eligible to this form if you have been working and/or paying in to the UK system for the last three years prior to leaving the UK. The E106 provides cover for two years; thereafter you will not be able to request an extension. If, after the E106 expires, you have reached retirement age, you can then apply for the E121.

There are other countries with which the UK has a reciprocal arrangement and a full list of these and the various benefits available can be found at the Department of Works and Pensions website: **www.dwp.gov.uk/lifeevent/benefits/social_ security_agreements.asp**.

Drug carrying

If you are taking regular medication you should ask your doctor for a prescription for at least three months. Taking a good supply of your medication will give you time to locate a new doctor after settling in. Make a photocopy of the prescription so that you can give it to your new doctor.

Name that drug

The trade names of medicines vary around the world, so don't be surprised if you are prescribed something you don't recognise in your new country. If you are at all uncertain, ask the local pharmacist how your new prescription compares with the old one (another good reason for having a photocopy). He or she should be able to put your mind at rest.

Health draining wealth

Whatever your reasons for going, your health is something that should top your list of priorities when it comes to moving abroad. If you are not covered under the destination country's health service, or the standard of treatment is poor, you will need to consider purchasing health insurance.

Regardless of how healthy you are now, an accident or unforeseen illness could cripple you financially.

Getting the right cover

Don't jump at the first option you find. Take a good look around and ask lots of questions.

What to look for:

- A cost-effective scheme giving a full range of benefits.

- Pre-existing ailments covered.

- Easy to understand and use, with good assistance and a simple claim system.

- Affiliation with local facilities, hospitals, nursing care and doctors.

- English-speaking practitioners if at all possible.

- The option to be moved elsewhere (your home country, for example) for intensive and/or specialist treatment if needed.

Topping up

Even if you have cover under the country's health scheme you might find you have to pay up front and are only reimbursed for a percentage of your medical costs. If this is the case, you should consider taking a top-up medical cover plan. Although paying part of prescription costs might not break the bank, a stay in hospital could well do so.

Teething problems

Dentistry and optical work are often either not covered at all under a country's healthcare, or have ridiculously low thresholds at which the patient starts paying. Even if it appears that the healthcare is good and you are able to join the national scheme, do remember to ask if your gnashers and specs are covered. If they are not, a top-up option just covering these might be cost-effective.

Copies of copies

We've already mentioned the need for multiple photocopies, but when it comes to healthcare these become even more important. Regardless of where in the world you register for healthcare, someone will ask for photocopies of birth certificates, marriage papers and passports, and not having them in abundant supply often means having to return at a later date to complete the registration process. If you are moving to a country where English is not widely spoken, it is advisable to have notarised translations made – and then make copies of the copies.

What's up, doc?

If you, or any family members, have existing medical conditions that require ongoing treatment, or regular check-ups, ask your doctor and/or specialist to write a report that you can present to your new doctor. If moving to a non-English speaking country it is essential to have the medical reports translated by a professional.

But, it's my head that hurts!

Unless you are fluent in the native tongue it is a good idea to take along an interpreter. Sitting in a doctor's office is not the right time to try out your new-found language skills. You never know what might get examined in error!

It's an emergency...

Don't wait until an emergency occurs to find out how far the nearest hospital or clinic is from your home. Make it one of the first things you discover. Remember, health facilities (even in developed countries) can be scarce and/or inadequate in remote regions.

Expat trivia

A survey found that about 41 per cent of Britons who moved abroad were back in the UK within 12 months because of poor preparation for their new life.

Summary

- Have a full medical check before moving abroad.

- Buy extra contact lenses and/or an additional pair of glasses.

- Remember that travel insurance becomes invalid once you are a resident.

- Get a European Health Insurance Card for travel to Europe.

- Pensioners moving to Europe should arrange an E121.

- Take at least three months' supply of prescribed medicines.

- If not covered fully by the state take out health insurance.

- A stay in hospital can be financially crippling – take out top up cover.

- Dental work is often not covered by national health services.

- Have multiple copies of all certificates when applying for health cover.

- Ask your doctor for a written report for your new doctor.

- Have all medical paperwork professionally translated into the new language.

- Take a translator to the doctor with you if your language skills are not good.

- Find out where the nearest clinic or surgery is as soon as you can.

- Remember health care may be poor in remote regions.

Money matters

chapter 11
Money matters

Preparation is the key to making sure your finances remain healthy once you've moved country. Ignorance of the law isn't a crime, but it can be a disaster. Some legal and financial aspects of your new country will be different from those of the country you leave behind. But don't panic! Knowing which questions to ask makes finding the answers a bit easier.

Vive la différence!

Something to bear in mind, when considering your finances overseas, is that many aspects will be different from those with which you are familiar. If you anticipate this, it will make it easier for you to keep an open mind and guard against making errors by assuming safeguards are in place, when they are not the norm in that particular country.

Tax, tax and more tax

Tax is the curse that knows no boundaries. Rich, poor or in-between, working, retired or a bit of both, the tax man wants his share. So don't forget that you need to notify the Inland Revenue that you are moving abroad, or you could end up paying more tax than you should. Once you change countries you're dealing with more than one tax authority and you need to find out if you have any choice in where you pay, as it is sometimes possible to select your tax domicile.

Check with an accountant to establish whether your new country has a double taxation agreement with your country of citizenship, so that you can avoid paying twice on the same income.

You may have been filling in your own tax form for aeons, but it isn't advisable to do so when confronted with a foreign tax authority demanding their slice of your pie.

A time to quit

When to hand in your notice isn't necessarily a simple matter of giving the required notice period. If you quit at the right time, you might find yourself the recipient of a healthy cheque from the Inland Revenue.

PAYE employees who stop work without having reached the lower earnings limit for the current tax year (having only worked for a few months) might be eligible for a refund of the tax deducted.

And then still more tax

Apart from income tax there are many more taxes waiting to reduce your income. You need to find out what your contributions and/or liability would be towards social security, property taxes, capital gains, wealth and inheritance taxes. Invest in yourself by paying an accountant to look into these matters on your behalf.

Keeping a second property

You might have decided to keep your house, or buy a smaller place as a bolthole should you decide to return home. If so, this could have an impact on your tax status. If you let your home you will almost certainly be liable to income tax on the rent and selling it at a later stage could leave you open to a hefty capital gains charge.

You could also have tax problems in your new country if you cannot prove that the property bought there is your primary residence. In some countries an annual tax is charged on second properties. In most countries capital gains is levied on the sale of a property not deemed to be the primary residence.

It is necessary to discuss the tax implications with a tax advisor in your home country and also in the new one if you intend to keep two homes.

When to move?

Ask an accountant in your home country when would be the best time to stop being tax liable there. By leaving at the right time you could find yourself the recipient of a healthy tax rebate. If you are moving to a country with a lower tax rate the timing becomes even more crucial as you might be able to reduce your overall tax liability.

Some wills won't

You may have fallen out with your son or daughter and decided they'll not inherit a penny of your hard earned cash, but, if the new country of residence follows Napoleonic law, you cannot disinherit your children. Neither can you leave more to one child than to another. In these countries leaving your property outright (both fixed and moveable) to your spouse isn't possible either. There are ways around these issues, but it requires careful planning before buying property. In all cases, regardless of where in the world you settle, consult a local legal expert and don't take chances. You need to know if your last testament won't do what you hope it will!

Inheritance Tax thresholds

The threshold at which Inheritance Tax is payable can be much lower overseas than at home. In some countries it is as low as £10,000, which could cause serious financial hardship for a surviving spouse unless a plan was put in place (in the form of insurance, for example) to take care of the burden.

Plan your deeds

When it comes to deciding how you want to buy a property, whether in both names, one name, or in a trust, you need to have a clear idea of the property laws before making an offer. In many countries an offer is binding and a deposit becomes forfeit if the purchase doesn't go through due to the purchaser pulling out. The offer should be made in the names of the eventual owners – so decide how to buy before you even start looking.

Legal language

Unless your solicitor speaks English, or you are virtually fluent in the local language, always take an interpreter with you to all meetings where legal matters will be discussed. Never sign anything that hasn't been translated into English and that you are completely happy you understand.

Amazing as it may seem, many expatriates sign papers in foreign languages that they would never dream of signing in English without reading the document carefully from beginning to end.

You may be loath to cause offence, but it's better to insist on having the documents translated, than find out in a few months that you've signed all your rights away because the situation differs from what you'd been led to believe.

Voluntary contributions

If you have taken early retirement, or intend to work as a self-employed person, you might want to consider making voluntary contributions to enhance your final pension. Contact the International Pension Service at **www.thepensionservice.gov. uk/ipc/home.asp** and ask for a forecast to see whether making additional contributions would be of benefit in your particular circumstances. The higher your income when you eventually stop work altogether, the easier it is to enjoy retirement.

Frozen pensions

Ask your state pension service if your pension is going to be put on ice. It could have a negative effect on your finances if you live for a number of years in a country with a high rate of inflation, while your pension income is frozen at the same rate as when you first moved abroad.

Exchange can change

When you calculate your income to decide whether you can afford to live overseas, don't forget to factor in a wide safety margin. Even a small drop in the exchange rate can radically alter your retirement income, leaving you unable to enjoy the type of life you'd planned.

Bank on it

If you have any savings that you wish to leave in the UK and your bank account has the option to be classed as 'not ordinarily resident' you should be able to receive the interest without tax being deducted. Talk to your bank or building society and they will arrange for you to fill in an R105 form for the Inland Revenue.

If they're selling, don't buy

It's sensible to take financial advice from someone well-versed in the financial markets when you move. There may well be good investment opportunities, or things that look great on the surface, but should be avoided at all costs. As a newcomer to the country it will be almost impossible for you to know one from the other, so taking expert advice is necessary. But a word of caution – make sure the advice is impartial. If they are trying to sell you something else, even if it is unrelated to the investment suggested, they cannot be considered impartial or independent.

Offshore – not sure?

Regardless of which country you choose, if you have offshore investments, or are thinking of investing offshore, you need to take advice from someone with the necessary expertise. Start by making contact with your bank in your home country and asking them to put you in touch with a reputable company.

To get a feel for what is available you should visit several websites, so that you understand the language and are able to discuss possible investments without confusion. The sites listed below are possible starting points for investigating your options, but are not endorsed by the author or the publisher of this book.

www.expatfinancedirect.com

www.expatinvestor.com

www.icplanning.co.uk/offshore.shtml

www.investorsoffshore.com/

www.offshoreinvestment.org

www.shelteroffshore.com

Take advice and ask questions

You will have noticed that nearly all of the tips in this section tell you to ask advice of specialists in their field. The reason is simple – you are going to a foreign country, with different laws, taxes, customs, and possibly even a new language. There is no way you could safeguard your finances and do the right things without guidance. It's better to pay for good advice and keep your finances secure.

Summary

- Don't try to fill in your own tax form when abroad. It's worth paying someone to do it for you and might be cheaper.

- Allow for secondary taxes such as social security payments, capital gains, wealth, inheritance and property taxes.

- A second property could result in additional taxation. You could be taxed if your property is not your primary residence.

- Ask your accountant which month would be the best time to make the move as you could benefit from a tax rebate.

- Ensure your will complies with any inheritance laws. Leaving money to the cats' home might not be allowed!

- Inheritance tax thresholds vary. If you don't put a plan in place the surviving spouse could have a hefty tax bill.

- Property laws can be complex so take advice before purchase as you might need to set up a trust.

- Will your pension be frozen? The government doesn't give cost of living increases to expatriates in certain countries.

- Ensure financial advice is impartially given. People asking you to invest or selling you a house are rarely impartial.

- Offshore investments need specialist advice, so consult with recognised experts and read on the subject before investing.

- If you have to consult with a lawyer, a bank manager or investment advisor and you don't speak the language take an interpreter with you.

The final countdown

Make sure everything is ticked off your list. Have you:

- Completed your home inventory?

- Checked with your shipping agent that all paperwork is in place?

- Requested visas, permits and other legal requirements?

- Had any necessary vaccinations?

- Collected all important documents such as: passports, tickets, certificates (birth, marriage, professional), visas and permits, in one place so that they are not packed in error?

- Made photocopies of all important documents?

- Organised online access to bank and credit card accounts?

- Notified everyone on your contact list?

- Organised a mail re-direction?

- Labelled all the spare keys?

- Arranged interim health insurance?

- Had medical, eye and dental checkups?

- Had translations made of medical notes?

- Collected sufficient medications to see you through the first few months?

- Organised pet transport and passport?

- If necessary, stocked up on pet items such as worm medicine and flea products?

- Set up a Skype or other Internet telephony account?

- Set up a roaming email address, such as hotmail?

- Fitted new plugs to household appliances, or bought adapters?

- Disposed of flammable items and anything banned by your new country?

- Drained fuel from lawnmowers and power equipment?

- If necessary, had the satellite dish removed?

- Taken final readings of utilities?

- If driving, planned the route from door to door?

- Made a note of any emergency numbers you might need on the journey?

- Organised temporary or hotel accommodation for when you first arrive?

- Written out useful phrases to show to people in case your accent lets you down?

- Given the removals driver an emergency contact number?

Useful contacts

Pet transport and regulations:

Airborne Animals: **www.airborneanimals.com**

DEFRA help for guide dogs:
www.defra.gov.uk/animalh/quarantine/pets/procedures/support-info/assistance.htm

Dog friendly companies:
www.dogfriendly.com/server/travel/info/customs/travelcustoms.shtml

EUROPA — Questions and answers concerning PET passports:
http://ec.europa.eu/food/animal/liveanimals/pets/qanda_en.htm

Fly Pets: **www.flypets.com**

Guide Dogs: **www.guidedogs.org.uk/index.php?id=2245**

Jet Pets: **http://jetpets.com**

Le Dog Stop: **www.ledogstop.com**

Pet Express: **www.petmove.com**

Pet friendly airlines:
www.petscanstay.com/pet-friendly-airlines/airline_pet_regulations.html

Pet Travel — worldwide travel guide for pets:
www.pettravel.com

PETS – Air routes of approved EU and Non EU
charter companies:
**http://www.defra.gov.uk/animalh/quarantine/pets/
procedures/support-info/charter.htm**

Healthcare and health insurance:

All Nation Insurance Company: **www.allnation.com**

BUPA: **www.bupa.com**

Expacare International: **www.expacare.net**

Expat Financial: **www.expatfinancial.com**

Expat Health Centre: **www.expathealthcenter.com**

Expat Health Insurance Directory:
www.einsurancedirectory.co.uk/Expat-Health-Insurance.php

Global Health Insurance: **www.global-health-insurance.com**

Healthcare International: **www.healthcareinternational.com**

Insurance To Go: **www.insurancetogo.com**

Inter-Global: **www.interglobalpmi.com**

Medibroker: **www.medibroker.com**

Expat websites:

British American Society:
http://www.britishamericansociety.com

British Expat Magazine: **www.britishexpat.com**

British Expats: **www.britishexpats.com**

Brits in the States: **www.britsinthestates.com**

Britworld: **www.brit-world.com**

Contact Expats: **www.contactexpats.com**

Easy Expat: **www.easyexpat.com**

Escape Artist: **www.escapeartist.com**

Expat Exchange: **www.expatexchange.com**

Expat Focus: **www.expatfocus.com**

Expatica: **www.expatica.com**

Expat Link: **www.expatlink.com**

Expat Network: **www.expatnetwork.com**

Expat.org: **www.expats.org.uk**

Expats Abroad: **www.expats-abroad.com**

Expat Radio: **www.expatsradio.com**

Expat Singapore: **www.expatsingapore.com**

Expats in Italy: w**ww.expatsinitaly.com**

Expat Village: **www.expat-village.com**

Expat Woman: **www.expatwoman.com**

Expat Women: **www.expatwomen.com**

International Living: **www.internationalliving.com**

Just Landed: **www.justlanded.com**

Living Abroad: **www.livingabroad.com**

Moscow Expat: **www.expat.ru**

My Expatica: **http://my.expatica.com**

Orient Expat: **www.orientexpat.com**

Transitions Abroad: **www.transitionsabroad.com**

Food glorious food:

British Corner Shop: **www.britishcornershop.co.uk**

British Expat Supplies: **www.britishexpatsupplies.com**

British Food Direct: **www.britishfooddirect.com**

British Food Online: **www.expatessentials.com**

Expat Essentials: **www.expatessentials.com**

Expat Direct: **www.expatdirect.co.uk**

Expat Shopping: **www.expatshopping.coop**

Scottish Food Overseas: **www.scottishfoodoverseas.com**

Xpat Shop: **www.xpatshop.co.uk**

British expatriate top destinations:

Australia:

Australian High Commission
Australia House
Strand
London WC2B 4LA
Telephone: (020) 7379 4334
Fax: (020) 7240 5333
Website: www.australia.org.uk

Canada:

Canadian High Commission
Macdonald House
1 Grosvenor Square
London W1K 4AB

Immigration & Visa Section:
38 Grosvenor Square
London W1K 4AA
General Enquiries: (020) 7258 6600

Immigration & Visa Information:
Telephone: (020) 7258 6699
Fax: (020) 7258 6333
Email: ldn@dfait-maeci.gc.ca
Website:
www.dfait-maeci.gc.ca/canadaeuropa/united_kingdom

France:

French Embassy
58 Knightsbridge
London SW1X 7JT
Telephone: (020) 7073 1000
Fax: (020) 7073 1004

Visa Section:
6A Cromwell Place
London SW7 2EW
Telephone: (020) 7073 1250
Fax: (020) 7073 1246
Email: visas.londres-fslt@diplomatie.gouv.fr
Website: www.ambafrance-uk.org

Ireland:

Embassy of Ireland
17 Grosvenor Place
London SW1X 7HR

Passport & Visa Sections:
Montpelier House
106 Brompton Road
London SW3 1JJ
Telephone: (020) 7235 2171
Passport & Visa Sections: (020) 7225 7700
Fax: (020) 7245 6961
Passport and Visa Office Fax: (020) 7225 7777/8

New Zealand:

New Zealand High Commission
New Zealand House
80 The Haymarket
London SW1Y 4TQ
Telephone: (020) 7930 8422 Chancery

Immigration Service:
General Enquiries: 09069 100 100
Fax: (020) 7839 4580 Chancery
Immigration Service Fax: (020) 7973 0370
Email: email@newzealandhc.org.uk
Website: www.nzembassy.com

South Africa:

High Commission for the Republic of South Africa
South Africa House
Trafalgar Square
London WC2N 5DP
Telephone: (020) 7451 7299
Fax: (020) 7451 7284
Email: london.general@foreign.gov.za
Website: www.southafricahouse.com

For a comprehensive list of websites and addresses of embassies for British nationals, go to www.fco.gov.uk and then either follow the link for UK Embassies Overseas or Foreign Embassies in the UK.

Spain:

Spanish Embassy
39 Chesham Place
London SW1X 8SB
Telephone: (020) 7235 5555
Fax: (020) 7259 5392

United States:

American Embassy
24 Grosvenor Square
London W1A 1AE
Telephone: (020) 7499 9000 United States Information Service
55–56 Upper Brook Street
London W1A 2LH
United States Information Service: (020) 7894 0694
Website: **www.usembassy.org.uk**

Other useful contacts:

Britons moving overseas:
www.direct.gov.uk/en/BritonsLivingAbroad/index.htm

Taking vehicles abroad:
Driver and Vehicle Licensing Agency
Telephone: 0870 240 0010
Fax: 0870 850 1285
E-mail: vehicles.dvla@gtnet.gov.uk
Website: **www.dvla.gov.uk**

Voting from abroad:
The Electoral Commission
Telephone: (020) 7271 0500
Fax: (020) 7271 0505
Website: **www.electoralcommission.org.uk/your-vote**

Travel advice:
The Foreign and Commonwealth Office
Telephone: (020) 7008 1500
Website: **www.fco.gov.uk**

Immunisations:
Department of Health
**www.dh.gov.uk/enPolicyandguidance
Healthadvicefortravellers/index.htm**

Passport Service:
Telephone: 0870 521 0410
Website: **www.passport.gov.uk**

Inland Revenue information:
www.hmrc.gov.uk/cnr/faqs_general.htm

Pension information:
Telephone: 0191 218 7777
Fax: 0191 218 7381
Website: **www.thepensionservice.gov.uk/ipc/home.asp**

Governments on the web:
Links to parliaments, law courts, city councils, banks and
government institutions for countries around the world.
Website: **www.gksoft.com/govt/en/**

Index

'The Greatest Tips in the World' books

Sex Tips
ISBN 978-1-905151-74-5

Travel Tips
ISBN 978-1-905151-73-8

Slimming & Healthy Living Tips
ISBN 978-1-905151-31-8

Wedding Tips
ISBN 978-1-905151-27-1

Tax Tips
ISBN 978-1-905151-43-1

Pet Recipe books

The Greatest Feline Feasts in the World
ISBN 978-1-905151-50-9

The Greatest Doggie Dinners in the World
ISBN 978-1-905151-51-6

'The Greatest in the World' DVDs

The Greatest in the World – Gardening Tips

The Greatest in the World – Yoga Tips

The Greatest in the World – Cat & Kitten Tips

The Greatest in the World – Dog & Puppy Tips

For more information about currently available
and forthcoming book and DVD titles please visit:

www.thegreatestintheworld.com

or write to:

The Greatest in the World Ltd
PO Box 3182
Stratford-upon-Avon
Warwickshire CV37 7XW
United Kingdom

Tel / Fax: +44(0)1789 299616
Email: info@thegreatestintheworld.com

The author

Lorraine Mace is a columnist with *Writing Magazine* (UK) and a regular contributor to *Queensland Writing* (Australia). A former humour columnist for *Living France* and *Spanish Magazine,* her work (fiction and non-fiction) has been published in the UK, America, France, Australia and the Republic of Ireland, as well as on the Web.

Winner of the *Petra Kenney 2006 Award* (comic verse category), she writes fiction for the women's magazine market, has been placed in several creative writing competitions, and is also a writing judge.

She is a tutor for the *Writers Bureau* and the co-author, with Maureen Vincent-Northam, of *The ABC Checklist for New Writers.*

www.lorrainemace.com